Praise for Empowered Communication

"Empowered Communication provides a perspective and set of tools that leaders need. We are putting them to work! The science is well-settled that people make decisions based on how they feel. Yet, most companies have a culture where emotions and personal issues are expected to be left at home. This is not the way to success in life or business. Susan Postnikoff provides invaluable insights into curating culture and emotions in business that, when practiced, lead to a flywheel effect between stakeholders, employees, and customers."

Jason Peterson, Chairman,
GoDigital Media Group - www.godigital.com

"Empowered Communication helps C-Suite Executives and Sales Professionals to combine traditional communication strategies with emotional intelligence and intuition. It is a must-read for all leaders wanting to drive their businesses beyond last year's levels of success to results that are currently unimaginable. Communication is the key to success, and Empowered Communication will lead the reader to unprecedented communication prowess."

Robert J. Moore,
Award-Winning, Best-Selling Author and Filmmaker

"Just when I thought all was lost, trying desperately to force my way past a veil of anger and frustration heaped upon me by my client, *"EMPOWERED COMMUNICATION"* rides to the rescue. Susan Postnikoff's wise and succinct work transports us to the virgin territory of compassionate listening and authentic interest; trading judgement for understanding and thereby crafting an auspicious encounter in a verdant field filled with the fragrant flowers of respect and appreciation; of Win/Win solutions to the most intractable of problems."

Clayton Norcross, Actor & Producer

"Empowered Communication is a fitting title for Susan's book, which does an incredible job with helping the reader understand and appreciate the significance of physical and mental balance. More importantly, it provides strategies for personal growth and development. This book is the perfect tool to help with building a plan for greatness."
Steve Lewis,
3 X Olympic Gold Medalist, 1 X Silver Medalist

"Susan Postnikoff has put in the time, the work, her heart, and her soul to create the powerful practices, tools, and skills necessary for having clear, honest, and intentional conversations where everyone genuinely feels seen, heard, and understood. When these practices are applied, your life will change for the better. Study this book.
Michael Bernard Beckwith,
Founder & CEO, Agape International Spiritual Center
Author, Life Visioning and Spiritual Liberation
Host, *"Take Back Your Mind"* Podcast

Empowered Communication
C-Suite & Sales Edition

Communication Tools to Empower the World's Greatest Leaders

By

Susan Postnikoff
International Best-Selling Author

Legal Disclaimer

Copyright © 2023 by Susan Postnikoff

EMPOWERED COMMUNICATION – C-SUITE & SALES EDITION

All rights reserved worldwide.

Dedication

This book is dedicated to my daughter Aliya. She has always inspired me to be a better person and to ensure that I go beyond my comfort zone to provide her with every opportunity possible. Remaining positive can be difficult during tough times, and remaining committed to the outcome while following one's instincts and passions will inevitably lead to success.

Foreword

You, the reader, are in for a real treat! Susan Postnikoff's book is much more than a few clichés on teamwork and communication – it's a deeply personal and paradigm-shifting introduction to the secrets to becoming a truly effective listener and beyond that, how to BE, in order to perform as an Empowered Communicator.

Susan has been a student of mine for decades, and with this book has taken the concepts and lessons I have taught her in communication and leadership, added her own wisdom and experience, and produced something that will most probably change your life.

This book goes beyond the basic 'how to' formulas for success to the essence of experiential learning, much more effective than just being told what to do or how to do it. Susan has added her own intuition and emotional intelligence to sound corporate judgement and scientific reasoning which sets this book apart and will allow you to be in touch with your own intuitive capabilities, a precursor to elevating your own leadership and communication skills.

The book will take you on a journey of self-discovery, which will result in an experience of true authenticity and ever-increasing leadership excellence. As Susan's proud coach and mentor, I feel she has created a unique and powerful treatise that will make an extraordinary difference in your life and in our world."

**Marcia Martin: Global speaker, Author,
Personal/Business Coach, and Corporate Trainer
www.marciamartin.com**

Chapter 1.

Communicating Responsibly

People look for who's to blame when miscommunication occurs. This book will result in both listeners and speakers understanding how to be responsible and accountable for their communication. While other books will tell you to focus on the speaker, acknowledge, build rapport, be authentic and don't interrupt, this book instills in you the skills to do so. It provides a very deep understanding of the listening process and builds the skills that are required to be engaged in conversation as a present, authentic, active listener.

This short but invaluable book will provide you with the tools and skills to converse effectively with anyone in any setting and to be able to speak confidently and impactfully to an audience of any size. You will be provided with rules, definitions and distinctions that will provide clarity on how to engage in authentic and effective communication that empowers you to produce action and results.

Effective communication is the most valuable tool we have in our society... in our world. It is no secret that to be an effective manager, it is necessary to be a powerful communicator. The number one complaint in any organization is poor communication. Even the advent of email, cell phones, text messages and the world wide web - with its plethora of communication apps - has yet to change the fact that business failures and losses are almost always a result of communication breakdowns.

Tom Peters stated back in 1987 in his book, Thriving on Chaos, "…a major reason for poor performance in American Management is the fact that managers don't listen to their employees, to their clients, or to what is going on in the market". We are now in 2023, and this lack of effective listening has yet to change. So, what is present, authentic, and effective listening, and how does one develop the ability to engage?

Empowered Communication is geared towards executive leadership and sales and is an essential read for anyone wanting to master effective and results-driven business communication. C-suite executives and sales professionals will find this book crucial to maximizing their success. While this book focuses on business, professional communication utilizes the same principles that need to be applied in every aspect of our personal, familial, and social lives.

Chapter 2.

Listening Defined

What most people think of as listening, is simply the biological function of hearing that the Merriam-Webster online dictionary defines as the, "…process, function or power of perceiving sound; specifically: the special sense by which noises and tones are received as stimuli." Hearing consists mostly of the physiological function associated with our ears and can also be enhanced by other physiological functions such as sensations of wind, temperature, and vibration. Some people are more intuitive and can sense energy associated with communication as well. I used to assist at volleyball camps for hearing impaired players, and we would hold a dance with every camp. Music was played exceptionally loud, so hearing impaired players could feel the vibrations caused by the sound waves. During volleyball drills we used sign language, facial expression, and body language to help communicate with the players. Every non-verbal form of communication that helped us communicate with the hearing impaired, also helps communicate with those that can hear.

The type of listening this book focuses on, is a listening that takes the physiological functions of hearing and adds the concepts of core beliefs and interpretation. As simple as that may sound, interpretation is extremely complex, and is different for everyone.

Our interpretations are linked to our individually accepted beliefs and are filtered through those beliefs as well as through our mood, experience, the context of the communication, and many other factors. Each individual listener will need to develop a specific skill set that allows them to better understand themselves, and then others, to effectively interpret the messages communicated to them.

The biological/physiological process of hearing is simply not adequate for effective communication. Only with a very deep understanding of each communicator's beliefs and interpretations can communication breakdowns be prevented, and complete messages be communicated as intended.

Listening Through Beliefs & Interpretation

With the use of email, text messages, video communication apps and voicemail, we clearly have the technology to record and confirm any message that was sent or received. So how is it even possible that miscommunication still occurs in business today? Given the frequency of miscommunicated messages, it is only logical, that we accept that what is still missing is an understanding of how we interpret the messages we receive. Additionally, the information we send is also filtered and affected by our own beliefs and interpretations. It is crucial that we become aware of how we each came to develop and adopt our current beliefs, and how we interpret new information through those beliefs.

Thinking Outside the Box

We have all heard the cliché, 'thinking outside the box', and there are a lot of sales professionals and managers that believe they think outside the box. I have noticed that some managers hire new employees with a value on recruiting people who think outside the box. Then, once the employee is hired, they are taught the current systems and processes, and if someone varies from doing things how they are instructed, they are often reprimanded for behaving insubordinate or challenging authority.

Why would a manager hire someone who is known to think outside the box if they are just going to shove them back into the box? What some managers have not realized is that 'the box' is inside each person's own head, and many people are subconsciously stuck in their heads… they are stuck in their thoughts and beliefs. Not everyone will have the same perspective on what is inside the box, versus what is outside.

When a manager is stuck inside their own head and are simultaneously convinced that they are an outside the box thinker, and the new employee thinks differently, they will devalue the new employee's perspective unless it matches their own. Ironically, it's when the new employee just does as they are told, that manager sees them as a like-minded, out of the box thinker.

There are leaders that truly appreciate fresh ideas and new perspectives. As such, they respond with wonder and excitement when presented with different ideas. Those leaders appreciate the value of unique perspectives, rather than being critical of them.

Getting Out of the Comfort Zone

In our comfort zone we generally know what to expect, and even if we know pain is coming, at least we know what that pain will be like, and that we have made it through that pain before. We have an internal knowing that we can survive it.

With a mindset of wonder and optimism we can make choices and take risks that create unexpected opportunities. Even though we cannot predict the new outcome as easily, we can be open to a possibility – a risk – that is more likely to produce joy than pain.

And even if that joy will require some change and growth, it is better than staying stuck in a state of fear, anxiety, depression, or disappointment.

Chapter 3.

Awareness

Most of us are moving about our communications like the proverbial bull in a China shop. The current pace of society and business has resulted in most people being in an altered state of consciousness, a state of hypnosis.

Hypnosis involves the induction of a state of consciousness in which a person becomes highly responsive to suggestion or direction and can be mentally programmed to respond in certain ways to specific stimuli. This is a perfect description of the average person going about their day while consumed by their thoughts and influenced by the constant bombardment of external stimuli from TV, billboards, radio, social media, etc. We are living in an advertiser's world, constantly receiving carefully planned and structured messaging that we subconsciously receive and react to. We are programmed by these ads to take certain actions in response to certain specific stimuli, and yet we are not consciously aware we are doing so.

I have a little bit of fun with this hypnosis technique in Beach volleyball – during a competitive tournament it would be considered unsportsmanlike conduct, and I would feel guilty and most likely end up missing my next point - but during fun games with close friends I use hypnotic suggestion to help score points against my opponent. The funny thing is, I will tell them what I am doing, and how I do it, and it still works.

For example, I will tell the opponent right before they serve not to serve the ball out of bounds. It plants the instruction, "serve the ball out of bounds," and most of the time, they do. Because the games are all in fun, they do not get mad at me. In fact, when I tell an opponent in a fun game, "Don't miss your serve!", they tell me to stop messing with their minds; and despite their awareness, it still works!

During serious games against a focused and determined opponent – someone in that Zen state – the technique does not work. At a more competitive level, against a seasoned athlete they are focused, and their awareness is heightened. Only if they are on an off day or for some reason have lost focus, will the blatant hypnotic suggestion work on a seasoned athlete.

The Mind Will Not Recognize the Word, '*Don't*'

This brings up the concept that our minds ignore the word, 'don't'. This is why when a coach, teacher or manager repeatedly says, "Don't do _____", the behavior they are trying to stop keeps on manifesting. For example, I was training for an AVP tournament, and my partner asked me to train with her and her coach. She and her coach had been working on getting her to pass the ball to the middle of the net, but having played professional indoor volleyball, she was used to passing to the far right.

During the session, the coach would get emotional and grimace every time she passed to the far right, and he would shout, "Don't pass to the right!" With all that energy and emotion, her mind kept hearing, "Pass to the right!" The coach needed to reinforce the skill he wanted, rather than what he did not want. "Pass to the middle" is the instruction he needed to implant into her conscious mind, and her subconscious.

It is not that he was a bad coach – in fact, he was and is a great coach! It was just that he and that athlete were stuck in a rut and did not have the awareness to recognize it in the moment. I suspect they eventually got past the issue, as the player did ultimately make the main draw, and signed her AVP Player Contract.

Any coach, manager or leader can find themselves in a rut. When they manage to get back to their center of balance, they will usually figure out the solution. The practices and exercises in Empowered Communication helps leaders, managers, and performers to return to their center of balance and find solutions quickly. The tools and methods in this book will save valuable time and revenue while eliminating frustration and creating joy and abundance.

The Root of Our Core Beliefs

Even if we carefully consider a decision for action, most of us are unaware of the root source of our own beliefs and the additional influences that affect our decisions for action. Most of us did not actually choose our own core beliefs. Most of us have subconsciously accepted our complex belief structure from outside influencers such as family, teachers, religious leaders, and the media.

We are also unaware of the beliefs and influences that are affecting the people we communicate with. The tendency is to assume everyone thinks the same way we do. In reality - during a conversation or presentation - each individual participating may have a different interpretation of the information communicated and may end up receiving a different message.

We want to believe we are right, so we tend to think, "Surely you would agree? Anyone can see this is how it is!" and we are nodding our heads in agreement as we unknowingly are walking away with different interpretations.

How do we come out of this state of hypnosis or subconscious reactivity and circumvent the programming we have adopted throughout the course of our lives? We must become consciously aware of our subconscious programming so that we can circumvent the reactivity and become effective listeners and empowered communicators.

Becoming Consciously Aware

Awareness is developed by objectively and subjectively observing both ourselves and others without placing judgment. Not placing judgement is crucial, as judgment is associated with our personal beliefs. Not judging allows us to be more open to listening, receiving, and considering the beliefs of others. If we judge, then we are behaving in a manner that indicates that we are attached to our own current beliefs.

One of the main purposes of self-observance is to re-consider our own beliefs and how those beliefs affect us. During the process of self-observance, we have an opportunity to consider the root-source of our beliefs and to then decide if those beliefs truly serve our best interests. Many of us are subconsciously holding ourselves back in our careers, relationships, communication, and spirituality by old beliefs that are no longer serving us. It is possible that our own tightly held beliefs are preventing us from achieving the success we desire.

Mindful Self-Observance

As we develop awareness about the beliefs and interpretations that are interfering with effective communication, we will open possibilities and solutions that we are completely oblivious to. We initiate our practice of awareness internally through mindful self-observance. The starting point of mindfulness is the observance of the little voice we each carry around in our own minds. Mindfulness focuses more on the observance and non-judgment of our own internal thoughts and beliefs, in contrast to awareness which starts from mindfulness and expands out to encompass the observance of our thoughts, actions, and interactions as we connect with other people.

As we become more aware of ourselves and our interactions with others, we become more attentive to the beliefs and interpretations of others. Mindful self-observance comes from a place of caring for others and being willing to set aside our own opinions as we explore the beliefs and opinions of others. It is truly a practice of selfless self-observance, and it is the first step in becoming a truly effective listener.

Mindfulness is based on our internal thoughts and imaginings, while awareness utilizes our senses and intuition to explore the world around us and to interact with that world. As our awareness expands, we initially start to observe ourselves participating in life and communication, and then we observe those communicating and interacting with us.

Approaching Zen

Ultimately, as we expand our awareness to a masterful level of observance and communication, we will be able to simultaneously observe ourselves, those we are interacting with, and others that they are interacting with. We will be able to see the entire playbook unfold in real-time for all the players involved. Then we can also perceive the potential for other people, entities, etc., to be affected by the players in their current actions, interactions, and communications. At some point, we will each develop a global and then universal perspective on how everything and everyone fits together and interacts, as we are all connected. This is approaching a Zen level of communication. We have started with the biological process of hearing, become aware of the effects of beliefs and interpretations, and are now also accessing our intuition.

Transitioning From Subconscious to Conscious Observation

As a hypnotist, when doing hypnotherapy, I am trained to take my clients deeper into a state of hypnosis by counting the client down from 5 to Zero, with Zero being the deepest state of hypnosis. When bringing a client out of hypnosis, I will count the client up from 0 to 5. "1,2,3,4,5 Eyes Open, Alert and Awake." With the recognition that most of us are already in a state of hypnosis, we can choose to count ourselves out and become more alert and aware in any moment in time. We can acknowledge that we are operating in a state that is less than fully conscious, and we can choose to count ourselves out of the subconscious or reactionary state into being fully conscious and deliberately responsive.

Exercise 1 – Declaring oneself to be "alert and awake"

The purpose of this exercise is to achieve a more conscious state of being.

i. Acknowledge being in a state of hypnosis.

ii. Declare that we will count ourselves out of hypnosis into a fully conscious state.

iii. Say out loud, "I choose to be fully conscious, alert and awake with my eyes wide open."

iv. Count and declare, "1, 2, 3, 4, 5 Eyes Open {open your eyes wide}, Alert and Awake!"

v. Note how you felt before the declaration and how you feel after. Has your posture changed? Has your breathing changed? Journal your observations about how you felt before and after the declaration.

vi. Do this exercise at least three times per day for one week.

Recognizing Opportunities

The more alert, awake, and aware we become, the more likely we are to recognize the opportunities that are available to us. With awareness, we can develop a more optimistic perspective and be more confident. It is easier to be confident when we have very clear perspectives on people, places, events, and opportunities. Clarity removes our fears and diminishes our hesitations. It allows us to focus on desired outcomes and to design plans that allow those outcomes to be achieved. Our obstacles become challenges, and our new-found courage and ambition kick in as we confidently set out to achieve our personal and professional goals. And, more importantly, when managers begin to operate at this higher level of awareness, they enable their staff and co-workers to expand their abilities and perform beyond expectations.

Confidence vs. Ego

Care must be taken not to confuse confidence with ego. One great tool to determine if you are truly confident or if you are operating from a more egotistical state is to notice if you are comparing yourself to others. The ego competes. A truly confident person wants everyone to win and recognizes the full potential in both self and others. The truly confident leader will maximize their own potential by bringing out the genius level in everyone they interact with — especially those on their teams at work.

The following is an example of how confidence and perception can have a very significant effect in a difficult situation. When my daughter was in grade two, she was being bullied constantly at school. Some of the teachers and playground staff did not believe she was being bullied because she was exceptionally tall for her age. She was literally a head higher than most of her classmates. Her best friend was the shortest girl, who was also being bullied.

When I brought up a situation to one of the other parents, without even listening to me, she cut me off and told me that my daughter must have been the instigator because she is so much 'bigger' than the other kids. That parent was stuck in the belief that taller kids pick on smaller kids. I talked to others about the situation, and someone recommended I take my daughter to Gracie Jiu Jitsu.

The Gracie Jiu Jitsu program had a history of helping kids that were being bullied. After my daughter was in the Gracie program for a couple of months, the bullying stopped completely. My daughter never had to implement any of the physical skills she learned. She never had to threaten the other kids with her new skills. It was not about the physical self-defense skills, but rather the confidence and positive energy she held.

Internal Voices

Cultivating mindfulness starts with the attempt to slow down that little voice that is constantly running in our heads. We start by acknowledging each thought and then releasing it. One thought at a time, we can acknowledge and release. Some thoughts may be valuable, some may be hurtful, and some we may be indifferent to. Set aside any judgment, just acknowledge each thought, and be at peace with it, no matter what it is. Just observe it.

What are some of the thoughts in your head right now? Perhaps you find yourself thinking, "What does this BS about mindfulness have to do with communicating and running a business?" "I don't have time for this S_ _ t!" or "Crap, I forgot to pick up the dry cleaning!" Many of us have multiple voices. What are some of the voices in your head? I have the procrastinator, the professor, the comedian, the knit-picker, the empath, the angel, and the devil all showing up in a single day. And did I mention the athlete, the lobbyist, and the judge? Oh, and don't forget the cynic!

Each of these voices exists for a reason. They are valid and, at times, helpful, and at other times they can move us off track or get us in trouble. Awareness allows us to observe these voices and choose which thoughts are worth acting on and which we need to release very quickly.

Exercise 2 – Journaling

i.   Start a journal for recording answers and results from this and other exercises in this book. Journaling on the exercises in this book will result in your expanded awareness about yourself as a communicator, a listener, and a leader. Expanding mindfulness and awareness starts with the senses and moves through thoughts.

Exercise 3 – Little Voices

i.   Listen to the voices in your mind and observe the thoughts that come to mind. Write down each thought in your journal and give a name to the voice that stated the thought.

ii.   How many different voices can you name? For each thought and the voice that is associated with it, in what way does it serve you? Does it provide protection? Does is give you courage or call you to action? Will acting on it have a desirable outcome?

iii.   There is a fine line between judging the voices and observing them. Try to simply observe them without judgment. Can you determine what thoughts are beneficial to your purposes and which may hinder you?

iv.   If there is a thought that hinders you, rather than judge it, just choose not to act on it. Just let it go. If there is a thought that serves you, you may choose how to utilize it and take appropriate action.

Exercise 4 – Visualization Meditation

i.   Get into a comfortable seated position.

ii.   Close your eyes and focus on your breathing. Slow your breathing to a calm, relaxing rhythm.

iii.   Imagine a place where you feel calm and peaceful, such as a beach, a forest, or any place that has been calming for you. It may be somewhere you have been or somewhere you would like to go in the future.

iv.   Use all five senses to add as much detail as possible to your visualization. What colors do you see? What is the setting? Are you outdoors? In a safe and warm home? At a beautiful resort? On a private island? What do you hear? Do you hear leaves rustling in the breeze, or birds singing, or something else? What do you smell? Do you smell flowers blooming, freshly cut grass, or something cooking? What might you taste? Is your mouth dry or watering? What do you feel? Is there a breeze cooling your skin? Is the sun warming your face? Are you wrapped in the warmth of a blanket? Can I feel the texture of clothing, blankets, or other objects in the image? How clear and defined are the images? How intense is the experience? What mood or emotions are coming up?

v.   Journal about the experience, and the images you saw, sensations you felt, moods and emotions that came up.

vi.   Repeat this daily.

vii.   This repeated process will continue to expand your mindfulness and your ability to visualize and to get in touch with your senses. As a result, you will expand your internal awareness, which will prepare you to generate more external awareness.

Eyes Open Meditation

Thich Nat Hahn – in his audio program entitled, The Art of Mindful Living, talked about developing mindfulness by deliberately concentrating on every simple task we do as we do it. He talked about having complete focus and concentration on walking … just focusing complete attention on placing one foot before the other and observing how we take each step from heel to toe. He referred to this type of focus and attention as a form of meditation. He also talked about "stoplight meditation" when driving. Rather than being stressed about wasting time at a red light, he instructed his followers to take advantage of the opportunity to meditate on the light – with eyes open, of course!

Exercise 5 – Eyes Open Mindfulness Meditation

i. Choose one or two chores you do every day that, prior to now, you thought of as dull, monotonous, or tedious. It may be cleaning your house, brushing your teeth, driving to work, or doing yard work.

ii. Usually, while people are doing these chores, they are thinking about something entirely different at the same time. Perhaps while doing these activities, you listen to music or a podcast, or you talk to someone on the phone. For the next week, choose at least one such activity, and give it 100% of your focus and attention.

iii. How does your perception of the activity change when you give it 100% focus?

iv. After practicing this open-eye meditation for a full week, how does your ability to concentrate on work or studying or an athletic activity change? How much has your focus and concentration improved on your most important activities after having practiced this eyes-open meditation for a full week?

v. How much has your productivity at work or in your studies increased? Are you winning more games or experiencing other successes more frequently?

In summary, developing awareness is an ongoing commitment that starts with self-reflection and evolves into a way of being. We all tend to have moments of conscious awareness, as well as times when we are that bull in the China shop. With commitment and practice, it is possible to spend a much greater percentage of time in a state of conscious awareness.

Chapter 4.

Interacting with Others

Once you have completed the exercises on developing mindfulness with the eyes-open meditations, have spent time discovering and getting to know your internal voices, and have taken stock of your beliefs and the sources of those beliefs, you are ready to activate your awareness with respect to your interactions with others. It is time to utilize all of your senses as well as your intuition.

Intuition often shows up as one or more of those voices you just identified. The next step is to observe your interactions and communications with others and with the world around you. Start taking inventory of how you are behaving and communicating at home, during sports and games and extra-curricular activities, and during business communications. It's time to play the game of life and simultaneously observe your participation in every facet of your life.

Take inventory of your thoughts, your internal voices, and your conversations, actions, reactions, responses, feelings, and emotions. Are you tending to be responsive or reactive? What emotions are you experiencing in response to various situations? Are those emotions responses or reactions? Are you remaining cool and calm and observing, or are you being triggered and reactive? When people are triggered and reactive, they tend to be coming from a subconscious state. When one is calm and able to formulate an effective response, they are usually in a conscious, mindful state of being.

Regardless of how you are reacting, responding, feeling, or acting, you need to remain the observer. We all need to observe ourselves and those around us, and we need to pay attention to how they respond and react to us. By continuing to observe, you will increase the frequency and duration of being conscious and mindfully responsive; and you will be able to decrease the incidents in which you react subconsciously. Additionally, you will become more aware of how others respond and/or react to you in different situations, and you can start to be conscious of affecting others in a way that is more beneficial, dignified, and purposeful for yourself and for those you are affecting. Your choices and actions will become more deliberate and will open more and more opportunities rather than close them off.

How Do You Listen?

What is your current listening style? Would you describe yourself as an active listener, task-focused, analytical, relational, critical, purposeful, or spiritual? Do you accept the message at face value, or do you look for alternative meanings? Do you tend to interrupt frequently? Do you perhaps ask question after question and then listen for the anticipated answers like you are conducting an interview… or perhaps almost like an interrogation? Do you ever hijack the conversation to suit your agenda? Do you intentionally seek to build rapport by empathizing, parroting, or expressing responsive emotions? How often do you interject, pause, or seek clarification?

Most of these approaches to listening and engaging in conversations involve attempting to manipulate the conversation and the outcome. Rather than being present, aware, and open, people are often listening and conversing with some sort of judgment or planned response.

That judgment will interfere with one's ability to listen authentically and to truly hear and receive the full intent of the message. Many professionals – lawyers, doctors, sales reps, etc. – are taught to listen for cues and indicators. Salespeople are often taught to actively listen for keywords and phrases as cues to move the conversation or presentation toward a particular planned outcome.

Unfortunately, this training has been done in such a way that most people tend to listen through judgment. As I stated earlier in the book, judgment is tied to beliefs and as such will prevent one from truly receiving the intended communication or message. There may be an outstanding opportunity being presented that a listener misses completely as they carefully and actively listen for the answers they are anticipating.

As you become increasingly mindful of yourself, you will also become increasingly observant of others and of your interactions with and affect upon others. In any setting or situation where you want to make changes or improvements, you need to be very observant. The better you get at being a conscious observer of both yourself and others, the greater will be your capacity to truly listen for opportunities to impact and influence change and to achieve the goals you and your teams are striving for. At the highest levels of awareness, you will achieve those goals while simultaneously leaving a positive and impactful imprint on others and on the world.

Chapter 5.

Achieving Centre of Balance

Our center of balance is both a physical positioning of the body and a mindset. When we find our center of balance physically, we are in a physically ready position, which is most commonly taught in athletics or martial arts. The center of balance is a concept that is truly at the center of our success in every aspect of our lives. The previous chapter discussed observing when we are behaving and communicating from a state of subconscious reactivity versus a state of conscious responsiveness.

The concept and practice of being centered and balanced is a tool to help us recognize more rapidly what type of state we are operating in. By being in balance physically, emotionally, spiritually, and intellectually, we are much more able to meet any obstacle that life appears to throw at us without becoming reactive.

Leading a balanced life generally means that we are finding appropriate amounts of time for career, family, spirituality, recreation, and self-care. Being able to find your center of balance in the moment will lead to the ability to find balance in all aspects of life. No one is balanced all the time. We are all repeatedly falling off-balance and then returning to our center of balance. This practice is exemplified by walking. Walking requires one to go off balance and then regain balance. If we do not fall forward, we cannot walk forward. We must constantly allow ourselves to fall and then recover if we want to walk effectively.

Our goal is not to practice remaining in perfect balance but rather to be thrown off and then recover immediately. The faster we recover our center of balance, the greater our ability to remain mindful and aware. Never being thrown off balance would be a very rigid and almost lifeless experience. Being alive and participating in life includes being thrown off balance and then figuring out how to recover quickly.

We need to develop greater awareness about what throws us off. What type of situations are we able to easily recover from, and what causes us to get 'stuck' in an unpleasant mood? What triggers us to feel upset? What situations, words, phrases, environments might be triggering us to spiral down emotionally and fall off balance? What specifically causes emotional upset, such as anger, fear, sadness, or loss of control? We may also have things that trigger pleasant moods and emotions. What makes you happy, excited, enthusiastic?

We may get so excited that we act out in excessive cheerfulness. It feels great and is great, and at the same time, our reactions may not always be considered appropriate. If we are concerned about our reputation and are working to affect our reputation in a certain situation, even being off balance in the most cheerful and enthusiastic way might not be what we want in that moment. The phrase that comes to mind is, "Please contain yourself." One of my middle school teachers used to say this virtually every day whenever a student got a little too boisterous. It can be just as inappropriate in a business or social setting to be uncontrollably cheerful as to be angry or hostile.

Our practice of being balanced provides us with a heightened ability to recognize when we are being thrown off no matter what the situation, and to regain balance quickly, to ensure we remain in control of our actions, thoughts, words, emotions, and identity. Through awareness, we can consistently demonstrate integrity and uphold our values and ideals. And, at the same time, we are also able to be present and available for others and to allow others to live their own truths, integrity, and values. We can be at peace with ourselves and simultaneously with others, even though we may not agree on everything.

It is very important that we remain secure in our own individuality while simultaneously allowing others that same experience for themselves. It is this equal or equitable acceptance of ourselves and others, combined with the interest and enthusiasm to learn about each other, that truly allows us to participate fully and altruistically in the human experience. This allows us to connect more deeply and personally with others and to approach our interactions and relationships with a sense of awe and wonderment rather than judgment when faced with differing perspectives and values.

Life Gets in the Way

Sometimes we have a major event coming up at work, and we need to put some extra time and effort in at work. During the time leading up to the event, our families and other important aspects of our lives may be intentionally put on hold while we prepare for the event. Likewise, there may be a personal event, such as a marriage, or perhaps a health issue that causes us to choose to put our career on hold for a while.

It is okay to temporarily shift focus, as long as one does not get stuck. This temporary shift in focus on work or in our personal lives can be advantageous. The work event may lead to a promotion or new business success, and it is also important to make our families a priority when marriages and other personal events come up. When we need to change our daily activities to prepare for a special event or handle a life crisis, it is important to communicate effectively with anyone who is being affected by the shift in our usual activities or responsibilities. During these times, while we are off balance in our daily lives, we will also have more moments of being subconsciously reactive or triggered. Our family members will need to be informed when we are going to spend some extra time at work, and work, of course, needs to know when we have a personal event affecting our professional availability.

Even when the special event is a happy one filled with excitement and joy, such as a marriage or a holiday, the change away from our usual activities alters our balance and is experienced as a form of stress. Keep this in mind the next time you find yourself fighting with a spouse or relative at Thanksgiving or Christmas! It might be a joyful fun time of year, but when one is out of their daily routine, that can cause unanticipated stress and may result in conflict.

Being in the Zone

In addition to being in a subconscious reactive state, or conversely a state of being consciously responsive, there is also an altered state of consciousness that is frequently referred to as being "in the zone". Being in the zone typically describes an athlete at the top of their game or a musician who is performing from a state that is more spiritually inspired.

Anyone may, at times, be in this altered state of exceptional productivity that can be thought of as a 'Zen' state; or is seemingly 'above' the conscious realm. Another description of this might be 'hyper-consciousness'. Whatever you want to call it, it is a heightened state of awareness where one is centered, aware and connected. It is the culmination of the practice of mindfulness and awareness that results in one being connected internally and externally to all that is – to others, to the world, and in a state of being able to perform, interact, observe, redirect, react and respond simultaneously, effortlessly, and impeccably.

The practices of mindfulness, awareness, and easily returning to one's center of balance will lead to one entering the Zen state more frequently and for a longer duration. We start by working on being internally mindful, then progress to increasing our awareness and ultimately graduate to entering the state of Zen.

When we are in that Zen state, we have the capacity to observe without being focused on the result but rather by simply allowing ourselves to be in the moment. In the realm of communication, in this Zen state, we are fully present and connected to our audience. We can speak when appropriate and listen and observe how well the information is flowing to and from us. We can be present in the conversation, and without the fear of forgetting something important, we can truly listen.

In writing this book, one of the most difficult decisions to make was whether to start with the concept of awareness or with the center of balance, as both practices work together. One will not succeed without the other. The more aware we are, the faster we recognize when we fall off balance, and the more balanced we are, the higher our level of awareness. Thus, we must work on both practices simultaneously. By mastering both practices, we will achieve a state of Zen more frequently. By being balanced and aware, we will recognize new opportunities, make great decisions, take the right risks, and speak, act, and behave with dignity, respect, integrity, and honor while being in harmony with others and the world around us.

Our Listeners' Listening

It is crucial that we authentically listen for our listeners' listening. Being in a high state of awareness provides the opportunity to communicate in conversation or as a presenter while also being an observer of ourselves and others. With that practice, we will develop the power to receive, to give, to comprehend, and to redirect as needed.

Practicing Centre of Balance

Being physically balanced means that one can remain motionless without effort. One is neither leaning forward, backward, nor to one side. By being relaxed with the natural curvature of the spine allowing one to simply stand still, with their feet approximately shoulder width apart, and at the same time being vertically balanced with the center of gravity secured so that a force from any direction will not allow one to be easily pushed over.

If a force (be it physical, emotional, spiritual, or intellectual) throws us off, we can either choose to hold our position or easily flow with the force and then just as easily return to our balanced position.

By being intellectually balanced, we avoid making incorrect assumptions and will notice if someone else is misinterpreting our message. By being emotionally balanced, we can avoid being triggered, and we will notice if someone else is being triggered. Being spiritually balanced in the domain of listening is not about religion but involves being in integrity and having the capacity to feel connected to something greater than ourselves.

Who Pulled the Trigger?

I want to point out that being triggered is an internal process – no one 'does it to you'. Someone may be triggered by something you say, and that is their response. If I am holding my center of balance and am in a consciously responsive state of awareness, you do what you do or say what you say, and I will receive it. Once I receive it, what happens to me and comes from me is dependent upon my internal beliefs and interpretations.

I may experience an extreme emotional reaction, or I may not. If I blame you and say that you have triggered me, then I am not taking accountability for myself, and I am not effectively managing my interpretations. If I were centered and aware, it is unlikely that I would be triggered. I would simply respond with wonderment at what you did or said, regardless of whether I liked it or agreed with it. And if I felt myself experiencing an intense reaction, I could then choose to consciously consider my own reaction and what may have caused me to have that reaction.

I can choose to maintain the power to reflect and respond. If I blame you for triggering me, I have given all my power over to you, and I am now playing the victim. A much more powerful response than blaming you for triggering me would be to consider the context of the situation and how it made me feel and then have a conversation with you about that. I can ask you what you meant and then engage in a dialogue that might be empowering for both you and me.

If I make a comment that offends someone – believe me, it's happened – although my intention was not to offend, I can respond with compassion and offer an apology. I don't know what I don't know, and it is easy to unknowingly say the wrong thing and upset someone else.

If someone becomes triggered, the best thing I can do is to allow them to be offended and avoid making them feel wrong for it. I may very well owe an apology, and after allowing them to bite my head off for my blunder, I can offer a sincere apology and an opportunity to dialogue about the upset.

As the one triggered, as hard as it might be in the moment, taking a deep breath and considering that the speaker may not realize the implications of their words, asking for clarification or offering insight is a much more powerful position than retreating like a wounded animal or retaliating with an intentional counterattack.

Where Does Your Message Leave Others?

For clarity, I am not saying that no one will be triggered by what you say or do. I am simply pointing out that anyone standing in their own personal power would not blame you for triggering them. I am also not saying it's okay to go around offending people — you will lose friends, get fired from your job and develop a horrible reputation.

It is very important to be aware of where your communication leaves others. You must have the awareness and compassion to handle the situation if someone is triggered by something you say. The differentiation is that anyone has the power to be responsible and powerful in taking accountability for how they react or respond. And at the same time, we can also choose to be responsible and accountable for how we affect others. We will all be triggered in moments of weakness. We will all need the compassion of another at times. What we don't want to do is to give away our own personal power or take it from another.

Society Needs Humanism

The willingness to discuss differences in beliefs and interpretations and the implications of those is what humanism is all about. When we develop the ability to consider the perspectives, intentions, beliefs, and interpretations that affect our racial, political, and religious debates, we will be able to reverse the polarity that has become so divisive in our current society. In fact, for decades, it has been considered bad manners or bad etiquette to discuss race, religion, and politics, but how will we resolve problems and reverse polarity if we cannot find a way to engage in sincere and humanistic conversations about these issues?

Being balanced and aware allows us to listen and respond rather than react. This allows us to consider other perspectives despite our own opinions and beliefs and to remain unattached to being right or wrong. Being spiritually balanced means being connected with humanity and accepting that we are all valid, we all have a right to our point of view, and we all need to be open to considering the perspectives of others without having to give up our own opinions and beliefs.

We must always come from compassion. I know there are times when people are simply not nice and say things to offend, but I do believe that most people, most of the time, truly have good intentions. They are simply not aware. Those of us who have done the work and have had the good fortune of receiving this type of training must offer compassion to others and help them to also become more conscious, balanced, and aware.

Emotional Intelligence and Intuition

In business, people are often expected to be logical and analytic to the extent of behaving like robots. We are asked to leave our personal lives behind along with our feelings and emotions. However, we are not robots. We are human, as are our coworkers — well, most of them – AI is changing that a little! For the most part, our employees, clients, and bosses are human; and there can be a huge disconnect when we are not spiritually balanced.

Being spiritually balanced means that we are consciously choosing to connect with humanity, and this allows us to access your emotional intelligence and intuitive abilities. By being consciously awake, alert, balanced and aware, we can communicate on a deeper and more authentic level. And we can be the player and the observer noticing our own actions and reactions, moves and responses, as well as those of others. And then, we can spontaneously and intuitively respond appropriately to produce the best possible outcomes.

Receiving Criticism

People are frequently triggered by criticism. It can be very difficult to receive information about yourself that is seen by another as imperfect or even 'bad'. When we receive criticism that does not feel good, it is very important to consider why it doesn't feel good.

When you feel yourself getting upset – perhaps your shoulders come up or your jaw clenches – ask yourself why the criticism matters to you. Our reputations can be shaped by criticism from others, so it may be important and useful information if the person it comes from has influence over you in a particular domain. I like to think of criticism as giving me an opportunity to be the 'fly on the wall' who gets to observe how others perceive me. I can then consider the information and where or whom it came from and then decide if I need to address it. If the information cannot really have any effect on me or on my reputation or identity, then it may be best to realize that it's just not important, and I can let it go. But if it can affect my personal or professional life, I may need to address it and respond to it.

By being aware and in balance, it becomes easier to respond appropriately and not to react inappropriately or irrationally. This is where meditating every day and developing one's awareness and ability to be consciously responsive, becomes particularly important. Criticism can be an asset if received, processed, and responded to effectively.

At some point, you will be ready to receive and utilize this type of information to your advantage as you develop new competencies and start to actively participate in building your identity. Without receiving and utilizing this type of communication, you would not have the same ability to transform how you are perceived by others.

This type of critical feedback is what gives you the power to produce the identity you desire, and in doing so, you will open opportunities for career, as well as for improved relationships and performance in the domains of your choice.

As you become more balanced and are more mindful, aware, and open to new possibilities, you will respond to this type of critique with wonder and awe as you quickly see the potential to utilize the information rather than be triggered emotionally by it.

Present Listening

This conscious state of being in balance and aware of the power of the unity of mind, body, spirit, and emotion is where we find the capacity for authentic, engaged, and present listening. This is the state in which we listen with our entire being rather than just biologically hearing a message. In this state, our personal and business relationships will flourish as our emotional intelligence and intuition are activated and utilized to benefit ourselves and others. And it is through benefiting others that a person or business truly achieves its greatest success. As stated by Tom Peters, *"Business exists to enhance Human wellbeing."* Without a product or service that others find highly valuable, sales revenue will never meet expectations. If you don't effectively listen to your customers, to your employees, to everyone involved in the process of delivering your product or service to customers that value it, your business will fail.

Trust Your Memory

Being able to meditate is a great indicator of your ability to become a powerful listener. You must develop the ability to trust yourself to remember important thoughts that come up, even as you let them go. When you are in a conversation, and an important thought comes up, you may want to interrupt the conversation for fear of forgetting the thought.

But to be a listener and masterful communicator, you must be able to listen and trust that any important thoughts you have will still be available to you when it is appropriate for you to respond. As you develop the ability to be centered and aware, your memory will also be more effective, and your fear of forgetting what you need to say will disappear.

Exercise 6 – Centre of balance for the body:

This exercise starts with finding physical balance - either seated or standing.

i. Near your belly button is your center of gravity or your physical center. For men, this tends to be a little higher than women due to men having broader shoulders and women having fuller hips. This center of balance is three-dimensional. From left to right, and front to back, this center is deep within our belly. When we physically position ourselves with our weight centered in three dimensions, we become physically balanced. The lower we can bring our weight vertically, the more easily we can maintain our physical balance. That is, at least until we try to bring it so low that we are not able to stay centered front to back and side to side due to other physical factors such as muscle strength and flexibility.

ii. Either standing or seated, find a position where you feel balanced so that you are not leaning in any direction and that you feel you could constantly and almost effortlessly hold that position for a prolonged period of time.

iii. If you have a partner nearby, ask them to try to gently push you from any direction, and note how well you can maintain your physical balance.

iv. Note that if you are tending to lean or fall forward, this may be an indication that you are tending to live for the future, and if you are tending to fall or lean backward, you are tending to live in the past. Remaining physically balanced keeps you more in the present, and it can help prevent you from falling off balance intellectually, emotionally, or spiritually.

Exercise 7 – Meditation to enhance spiritual balance:

One of the simplest forms of meditation is to simply sit still and observe your own breathing.

i.   Sit comfortably and physically center.

ii. Pay attention as you breathe in and then out. Is your breathing deep or shallow? Fast or slow? Are you breathing through your mouth or nose? How has observing your breathing affected your breathing? Do you find yourself breathing slower or faster as you pay attention?

iii. With a notepad at your side, note the time, and then gently close your eyes and meditate on your breath. The purpose of the notepad is to jot down any thought that comes up that you believe is important and are afraid you will forget. The goal is not to interrupt the meditation, but the reality is that it will be very difficult to focus on the meditation if something important comes to mind that you will worry about forgetting.

iv. Now, sitting centered with your eyes closed and listening to your breathing, mentally note when you start to lose focus on your breath, and then look at the time on your watch. How long were you able to focus on your breath before allowing other thoughts to come in?

v.   Now allow yourself to begin the meditation again, and as thoughts enter in to distract you from your breathing, mentally note each thought, release each thought, and immediately refocus on your breath. How long are you able to meditate without opening your eyes, stopping to take care of a new task, or to write down a thought?

vi. Continue to repeat the exercise for at least 10 minutes every day. Any time you find yourself feeling stressed or anxious is a great time to practice this meditation.

Chapter 6.

Interpretation and Miscommunication

As individuals, we are each listening and interpreting information through a very complex set of filters and beliefs. Because of this, we all process and store information differently. This applies to information we see, hear, and read. In this chapter, we will explore how our beliefs were formed and what filters we may be listening and communicating through.

Beliefs, Values and Culture – Our History

Many of our core beliefs and values were passed down to us from our elders and accepted by each of us as individuals at a fairly young age. The sources of our beliefs tended to come first from our parents and family, then from church, school, and other adults in our community who played a significant role in our lives. Our beliefs often stem from the rules that are imposed upon us by our government, religious organizations, schools, and families. These rules may change over time, and depending upon our life at the time, some of us may have been more in tune with those changes than others.

Some of us may have also been influenced to accept or reject such changes. As we grow older, our beliefs may change and expand. The more open, aware, and connected we are, the more likely we are to re-evaluate our beliefs.

If we grew up with families and communities that welcomed change, we likely became more open to change, and if those families and communities were resistant, we may have remained resistant. On the other hand, some of us may have an innate tendency to follow authority, while others may tend to challenge authority.

When we attend college or enter the workforce, we come across a new set of authority figures that influence our beliefs. We may also expand our beliefs through exploration of religion, through reading, through the media and through our interactions with others. Different religions teach beliefs and values that members of the religious organization are expected to agree and adhere to.

The era or generation we were born into, the history of our ancestors, our nation of origin and our personal race and religion shape our beliefs and values. We may also have some personal or individual experiences that were very significant in our lives, and those significant experiences affect our beliefs and values.

Interpreting Experiences

Each of us as an individual growing up even in the same community at the same age and in the same era will have had some different influences. Being male or female, being of a different race or religion, and connecting more closely with different people will cause each of us to interpret the rules and adopt differences in our beliefs. Even in the same community, in the same country during the same era, we all still experience life differently.

By developing an awareness about how differently we may have received information and experienced relationships, rules, and authority from birth till today is crucial. This understanding helps us to understand how the many differences we have, that are not apparent on the surface, but have shaped our beliefs and values from birth until today. This awareness will continue to influence our interpretation of messaging received and shared in communication now and in the future.

I do believe that most humans share a consistent set of basic needs, such as food, water, shelter, and love. Beyond those basic needs, we all have our own desires and priorities for ourselves and our families, friends, and communities. I cannot emphasize enough the importance of realizing that while in many ways we are all very similar, we do have perhaps even more differences. It is these very differences that truly make us each valuable as individuals. Without these differences, we would all just be clones of one another, and life would be extremely boring. Our individuality gives life color and vibrancy. The joy of communication is often the challenge and the excitement of identifying these differences and utilizing them to our advantage in our personal and professional lives.

Filtering Communication

By understanding how each of us has developed our own personal set of rules, beliefs, values, and experiences, we can start to understand the source of our communication filters. In addition to our cultural and personal history and how we each interpret that for ourselves, our communication is also dependent upon context and setting, personal commitments, mood and emotion, and health and fitness.

Context

Context is situational. It is the frame of reference within which the communication is taking place. In business, it may relate to a specific project or area of business that we need to discuss or that is being presented. Most people grasp the importance of context quite easily. Context is seeing a different point of view depending on the situation.

Responsibilities

We all have a different set of personal commitments, responsibilities, and considerations. We may be members of groups and churches for which we have made commitments. Most of us have commitments to family members, including parents, children, and spouses. We may be a member of a club or other organization for which we have made promises. Others may have considerations relating to their values, ideals, morals, and integrity.

Health

Health and fitness may affect one's filtering of communication as well. If one is in pain or has health issues, these will also affect one's listening and their priorities. When we are in pain, our ability to listen is impacted, as we may not concentrate as well. When we are dealing with the stress of a severe health issue – our own or that of someone we are close to – our ability to listen may be severely impacted. Our priorities will have altered, and our perception of what is important is not the same during a health crisis as it is when we are feeling great.

Mood, Morale, and Emotion

Mood, morale, and emotion can have a huge effect on communication. The mood and morale of individuals, groups, and teams within an organization can also shape the interpretation of personal, professional, and organizational levels. If someone is in a bad mood at work and feels disrespected, they may feel like they have limited potential to progress in their career. And conversely, one who is in a good mood may perceive a challenge as an opportunity to demonstrate their abilities and seek a promotion.

Moods are also contagious, and that one person with a bad mood can share it with team members at work, or family members at home. Moods are generally either positive or negative. Positive moods can include trust, ambition, confidence, acceptance, and optimism. Negative moods might include resentment, arrogance, resignation, and distrust. If a new training program is announced at work, and one responds with a mood of trust and optimism, they may be excited about the potential for new learning and advancement. If someone has a mood of distrust and resignation, they might view that same training as an indication that their supervisor believes they are inadequate or incompetent.

Other Factors and Experiences Affecting Interpretation

There are an infinite number of uncontrolled factors and unique experiences that can influence one's listening and one's perception during communication. Here is a list of some of those factors and experiences:

- Gender
- Race
- Religion
- Local Community/Culture
- Origin of Nationality
- Values and morals accepted by local, regional, national, and global community groups
- Laws – again, these may be local, regional, national, or global
- Family
- Education
- Health and fitness
- Career
- Trauma
- Awards
- Social groups
- The list may be endless!

We have all been shaped by our individual story. Throughout our lives, we have each accepted sets of laws, rules, or guidance as to what is good and bad or right or wrong. Each of us experienced a somewhat different set of circumstances, influencers, and even where we each fit into our own families was not the same. The story of my life and the story of your life are different. Even if we were twins, at some point, there would be differences. Even if we were provided the same information as we grew up, and we listened to the same stories passed on from our teachers, parents, and grandparents - or from history books - how we interpret that information today will be different for each of us.

We are all constantly receiving information and filtering and interpreting it for ourselves, and we may not realize that we are doing so. It is something we are each doing habitually and subconsciously. People who grew up in a free democratic society will have different interpretations than those who grew up in a communist society. People who grew up in a family with unlimited financial resources will interpret differently than someone who grew up in poverty.

Those who experienced race, religious or gender bias that limited their opportunities will see things differently than someone who has not been subjected to that type of bias. We have all had unique experiences that have shaped us as individuals, and we each end up with a unique set of accomplishments, confidences, insecurities, fears, and considerations.

How We Experience Reality

The reality we experience is different for each of us as individuals due to the different experiences and backgrounds that we have come through from birth – or perhaps even before we were born – until the present moment. It is extremely important that we develop a sensitivity to these differences leading up to any interaction or communication event. Center of balance, mindfulness, compassion, and awareness are the bases of developing this sensitivity. The more we determine to be intentionally present for others, the more sensitive and perceptive we will become to the reality others around us may be experiencing in the moment. And, adding the ability to connect genuinely, openly, and with compassion, enthusiasm, and wonderment will enhance our ability to experience, share in, and help shape reality for ourselves and others.

Exercise 9 – Revealing Beliefs and Interpretations

i. Consider past miscommunication events. How many times have you had the experience in a follow-up discussion where you find yourself in an argument of 'he said, she said' or a state of confusion about what was previously said? Perhaps you are being accused of saying something you did not say, or you are convinced someone else said something that they deny saying. Or perhaps following a group presentation, you and a friend or coworker who attended the same presentation somehow remember the content differently?

ii. List a few examples of these miscommunication events and write down a few key points from your perspective.

iii. Now, write a few key points from the other's perspective.

iv. What interpretations and beliefs might have affected your thinking?

v.   What differences in the other person's history, personal or professional experience, religious beliefs, mood, health, etc., might have led to their perspective being different?

By taking an inventory of our beliefs and interpretations, thinking critically about how our perceptions and inferences are affected by them, and then considering how others may have very different beliefs and interpretations, we can become much more aware of the potential for differing perspectives and points of view that may result in conflict and miscommunication.

By considering our potential differences and by also being centered and aware, we can consciously establish and confirm the correct context while giving or receiving communication. When we realize that we failed to prevent a miscommunication, we can resolve it by first clarifying the context and then if needed, consider any other factors and experiences that may have shaped the message in such a way as to have caused the miscommunication.

Chapter 7.

Identity and Reputation

A person's reputation is their identity as perceived by others. As stated by Marcia Martin, "Our identity in the world lives in the conversations of others about us." If we accept this statement to be true, we begin to realize the extensive power of communication. It is the most powerful skill we can ever develop. Our communication creates our reputation — our identity in the world. What we communicate – both verbally and non-verbally – defines our identity for ourselves and others, and our identity is crucial to our success in life.

Sigmund Freud theorized that most of our decisions are made subconsciously. This subconscious decision-making process is usually reactionary and results in our making decisions that are not congruent with the vision we hold of ourselves. It causes us to communicate with others in ways we have not intended. This causes us to create identities for ourselves in relationships and in careers that are not how we see ourselves. We tend to send the wrong message about ourselves. There is enormous value in learning to control and refine the messages we deliver about ourselves. How others perceive us will be influenced by how we allow ourselves to show up for others.

Communication is the key to success in our careers. As we become empowered communicators, we will produce exceptional results leading to increased revenues and growth. Being exceptional communicators also pays off in our personal lives.

Any opportunity to communicate effectively and lessen or eliminate the possibility of miscommunication paves the way for success and progress. With the ability to constantly observe ourselves as we live and play the game of life, we can affect our presence in the world. We become active participants, consciously building our reputation and identity, and affecting how others view and perceive us.

Self-Identity

Our first and most important identity is our self-identity. This identity lives in our own minds about ourselves and affects our self-image and self-esteem. Our self-identity determines how we allow ourselves to show up in the world for others. If we don't believe in ourselves, no one else will either.

External Identities

We all have multiple identities that form in the minds of others about us. For most of us, the second most important identity is our career identity, as this shapes our professional potential and success as leaders and influencers. Other identities that have a significant influence on our lives might be our family identity, political identity, religious identity, or our identity in extra-curricular settings. One of our first external identities is shaped by our family. Then we go to church, to school, to the gym, and to work. In every social setting we enter, we may develop a new identity. Have you noticed that your friends perceive you as having a different set of skills and abilities than your family does? Your identity at work may be completely different than your identity at home or at the gym or in a nightclub.

Exercise 10 – The Root of Our Beliefs:

    i.   Take a sheet of paper and write down the following headings:
  - a. Parents
  - b. Church/spiritual
  - c. School – teachers
  - d. Coaches

       e. Work/bosses

ii.   Under each of the above list items, list at least three beliefs that you hold as true.

iii.   For each belief, how has it served you? Does that belief support you in your life? Do you necessarily agree with that belief now? Is there anything you would like to change to make any of these beliefs more accurate for you?

iv.   Do you have any beliefs that do not serve you?

Exercise 11 – Discovering Personal Identities:

       a. Parents
       b. Church/spiritual
       c. School – teachers
       d. Coaches
       e. Work/bosses
       f. Significant events - such as accidents or injuries, marriages, divorces, children, loss of a loved one, winning a lottery, title, or award

i.   Under each heading, write a paragraph to describe your identity in that group or domain. Are there any people you interact with in each of these settings who do not appear to view you in a manner consistent with your perceived identity? If so, I encourage you to have a conversation with them about how they view you. How do they see you, and what events shaped their perception of you?

ii.   For each identity, how has it served you? How does this identity held by you - or by someone else about you - affect you in any way, either for the better or with negative consequences?

iii.   Do you need to take action to shift your identity in any setting or with any individuals (co-worker, boss, spouse, parent, friend)?

Shifting One's Identity

Communication is how we shift our identity. We can shift our identity in any setting by affecting the conversations with and by others about ourselves. We do not need to alter our identity in every setting or group that we engage with. We need to work on altering our identities in the domains that matter the most. If you are not achieving the career you desire, you may need to shift your reputation at work. If you have conflicts in your relationship with your spouse or family members, and you feel misunderstood, you may need to explore and affect your identity at home.

Chapter 8.

Altruism

On January 22nd, 2023, a friend of mine passed away. I dedicate this chapter to the memory of my friend Harry Cartwright. His passing was a sudden and unexpected loss of a person who lived in that space of balanced, aware, and altruistic love. On the day of his passing, some of his close friends held the first of many gatherings that celebrated his life and helped us cope with his loss. Harry was truly a central fixture of our community, and his impact was felt by everyone who knew him.

Self-Actualization

That night one person asked me, "You knew he was actualized, right?" And although I knew exactly what he meant; it made me think about what it really means to be self-actualized. Self-actualization is the process by which an organism or person realizes its full potential. The concept was first introduced by the Gestalt psychologist Kurt Goldstein in his 1939 book The Organism. It was soon adopted and developed by several early proponents of the humanistic psychology movement, such as Carl Rogers (1902–1987), the founder of client-centered therapy. Self-actualization today is most strongly associated with the work of Abraham Maslow (1908–1970), another early humanistic psychologist, and the creator of Maslow's Hierarchy of Human Needs.

When I think about Harry as self-actualized, I reconsider his language, communications, and behavior in a variety of settings. I also recalled my observations of his interactions and communications with others. Our identity lives in the conversations about us, and thus I also take into consideration what others said about him at his celebration of life, and on social media following his passing.

Here are some of my personal observations of a self-actualized person:

<table>
<tr><td>i.</td><td>he always showed up with a positive attitude, even during hard times</td></tr>
<tr><td>ii.</td><td>he always included everyone who wanted to participate in any event he hosted</td></tr>
<tr><td>iii.</td><td>he always talked about others in a positive, constructive, and beneficial manner</td></tr>
<tr><td>iv.</td><td>he did what he loved as a career, with no apparent concern over money</td></tr>
<tr><td>v.</td><td>he was married, and he and his wife had a committed and unwavering relationship</td></tr>
<tr><td>vi.</td><td>he had a belief in a higher power and was open about it</td></tr>
<tr><td>vii.</td><td>his compassion and unconditional love were always felt by those in his presence</td></tr>
<tr><td>viii.</td><td>he held meaningful deep conversations with people one-on-one, and he always managed to

find time to give every person in attendance one-on-one time and a hug</td></tr>
<tr><td>ix.</td><td>one person told me about losing his temper with my friend, and my friend's response was to put his arm around him and say, "We are going to work this out, and we are going to stay friends."</td></tr>
<tr><td>x.</td><td>The number of people his love and compassion affected extends beyond our ability to count</td></tr>
</table>

xi.   After his death, several people vowed to be more like him…more loving, compassionate, and inclusive with a zest for life

A self-actualized person – like Harry - is not triggered by things that would likely upset others. A self-actualized person is simultaneously calm while taking spontaneous action. That person remains in joy and wonder at the beauty of life regardless of what it appears to throw at them. They have a positive effect on others through a presence that is openly compassionate, loving, and powerful, with seemingly no ego. The self-actualized person never needs to be right, and yet it seems like they always make the best choices.

Chapter 9.

Authentic Communication

A great communicator can produce and invoke trust. A masterful communicator demonstrates authenticity in all communication and remains honest. The best way to invoke trust is to always be honest. The slightest 'white lie' that you are caught in, will plant the seed of doubt for all future communications. Even though we may have the most sincere and caring intentions, deception does not hold the deceived in a position of power or dignity. We may believe that we are sparing someone's feelings, avoiding a confrontation, or trying to avoid a troubling circumstance. This is a false narrative - a deception is never a masterful act of communication. As much as one may justify the deception as somehow being in the best interests of another, it usually only spares the perpetrator of the deception from being affected by the deceived person's reaction to the truth.

Information With Purpose

There are times when information is not pertinent, and sharing it serves no purpose. There may be situations where the context or setting are not appropriate. And there may be situations where sharing certain information serves only to do damage. Information that affects decisions that need to be
made by or with others should be shared. Information that will have no positive benefit and may cause shame, humiliation or loss of respect or dignity may be best left unsaid.

It is much easier to remember the real 'who, what, when, where, why, and how,' than to try and remember one little deviation from truth. The moment you deviate, you then need to remember that deviation and everyone and everything that was connected. Then you must remember who you told the truth to and who needs to know about that one little deviation. And inevitably, you will need to rely on someone else to take part in the deception. And this is how the dark spot on your integrity grows. Who was given the original version, and who was given the modified version? Who did each of them share the original and the modified versions with? The dark spot on your integrity will grow and fester until the day you either get caught in the lie or can no longer handle the looming feeling of having been dishonest. And if you ever find yourself spinning and dizzy in the perpetration cycle and want to escape its wrath, the only way is to come clean and tell the truth.

Lying intentionally by stating incorrect facts or by leaving out pertinent details will often result in breakdowns in communication. People who communicate honestly prevent communication breakdowns. In addition to intentionally telling a lie, being less than honest can also consist of leaving out key details that might alter the decisions made by participants in the conversation. This is generally considered lying by omission. Masterful communicators are confident in their ability to manage the interaction without having to leave out pertinent details.

Sometimes facts may be unintentionally misconstrued. At times it can be difficult to discern between truth and interpretation. Sometimes what seems like hard-core facts and accepted beliefs by one person or group may not be held as truth by another. We all have different backgrounds and experiences.

Even in science, there are often conflicting studies that simultaneously prove and disprove the same hypothesis. Becoming a masterful communicator requires that we be present, centered, connected and aware. It is important to remain open to other perspectives, beliefs, and values. Even with facts and scientific studies to back up our position in a discussion, we can win the battle but lose the war by allowing communication to break down when we refuse to consider another point of view.

Integrity

Integrity refers to a code of ethics that is in alignment with one's beliefs and values. A code of ethics may be agreed to by a member of a group such as a company, church, or family, and that can also include governments, cartels, and other groups with bad intentions. An individual may be a part of one group or of several groups and may agree to different codes of conduct with each of those groups when relating to, working for, or participating in each different group.

One's personal integrity is the code of ethics one lives by regardless of the groups to which one belongs. Having integrity means living by one's own code of ethics, even when no one is watching. Living in integrity allows everyone with whom you interact to know what to expect from you and to be able to depend on you to behave in certain ways and to make certain decisions consistently. It allows each of us to be seen as reliable, dependable, and trustworthy as well. There are some people whose code of ethics can allow certain perpetrations. The best example of this is a mafia or gang member whose personal integrity may involve breaking the laws set by the government or society. A more subtle example is the person who does not bother correcting a person if they misinterpreted something that was said when the situation would seem to make such a correction unnecessary.

I have a rather humorous example of going along with a situation where someone incorrectly heard me say something, and I did not think it was necessary to correct them. I had done an acting class and auditioned for several producers. After the class auditions were complete, there was a social. I met a young woman who introduced me to her boyfriend/producer. She looked like she was about 18 years of age, and her boyfriend was at least 20 years older, and she announced to me that she was an adult actor.

I wondered why she felt it was necessary to inform me that she was an adult – I was naive and did not know what the term 'adult actor' meant. As the conversation progressed, she mistakenly heard me say I had recognized her from one of her films, and she excitedly informed her producer/boyfriend that I had seen her in a film. Not wanting to embarrass her in front of her producer/boyfriend, I went along with her interpretation. She asked which film, and I simply said I did not remember the title (notice I had to tell an additional lie now to keep the first mistruth going).

It was about 20 minutes later that I understood what it meant to be an 'adult actor'. I found the situation hilarious, as I had been standing with an actress from the adult film industry and her boyfriend, apparently stating that I had seen her acting in one of her films.

For the two of them in that industry, this type of conversation was as uneventful as Tom Cruise talking about someone having seen him in "Top Gun", and of course, they wanted to hear that people had watched the film! But I was embarrassed and internally laughing at myself at the same time as I considered the couple thinking of me watching the young woman performing in that type of role.

Because our identity lives in the conversations of others about us, our integrity is demonstrated in those conversations. When we are in a group and are caught in a mistruth or perpetration, we may be shunned by the group and experience embarrassment. It may result in conflict between us and other members of the group. There may be negative consequences, and we may even be eliminated from that group. This may mean being fired from a job, disinvited from family functions, or being cast out of social groups. Some may end up in prison as a result. When we perpetrate our own integrity, there are also negative consequences.

Many of us are our own worst critics, and we will internally punish ourselves consciously or subconsciously. This may result in us feeling nervous or anxious, and we may develop manifestations of mental or physical disease. Perpetrations of our own integrity can have the greatest effect on our identity, as those closest to us can quickly notice that we are off-center or in a different mood.

In time, the people closest to us at work and in our family and social circles will notice the effects of our breached integrity and will begin having conversations about us with other family members, friends, and coworkers. These conversations may be written or verbal, and they will affect our identity in those groups and, ultimately in the world. Social media can take on a life of its own, and our identities and breached integrity may be rapidly magnified online.

Managing our integrity is an important factor in managing the conversations about us at work, and managing the conversations about us at work is crucial to managing our corporate identity. Managing our integrity in our social circles has a huge effect on what ends up on social media. Maintaining our integrity means being true to ourselves and in doing so, being truthful to those we interact with.

Keeping agreements and commitments, keeping our word, and taking care of ourselves and of our family, friends, and coworkers - as well as our environment and communities – allows us to remain in integrity. Taking care of ourselves means listening to our bodies and caring for ourselves physically, emotionally, and spiritually. Taking care of others means listening to them and doing our best to support them as individuals. Taking care of others and our environment and communities means listening to them and keeping our agreements and commitments in those domains as well.

Conflicting Values

Maintaining integrity is not always easy. The greatest challenge is that we may be involved in several groups, and those groups may have conflicting values, beliefs, and rules to abide by. Maintaining personal integrity may mean taking a stand, risking being unpopular, experiencing disapproval and taking part in a confrontation. The reward is inner peace and self-respect.

Additionally, by being in integrity with ourselves, we will ultimately become aligned with the people, places, events, friends, coworkers, family members and social circles that we resonate with and are able to grow and flourish in. This will allow us to have deeper, more meaningful relationships with family, friends, and coworkers. Additionally, we will end up with a much more rewarding career and social life.

There are some people, who can utilize any position or situation they find themselves in as an opportunity to serve others in a way that benefits everyone emotionally, spiritually, and physically. It may be my altruistic friend running social events and local volleyball tournaments, or it may be the philanthropist endeavoring to stop child trafficking. Anyone that is in integrity and holds humanistic values, will migrate to opportunities that allow them to thrive and to have a positive impact on those around them.

Exercise 12 – Assessing Personal Integrity

i.   Journal about an occasion in which you did or said something that for you was disingenuous. What led up to your choice to make that statement? What thoughts ran through your mind before, during and after the incident? Did you notice any changes in your level of energy, productivity, ability to sleep, and were there any health manifestations?

ii.   How often do you find yourself meeting your deadlines, keeping your promises, and remaining true to your agreements and commitments?

iii.   How do you feel when you keep a commitment or agreement? If you had a situation where you wanted to break the agreement but did not, how did you feel afterward? What manifestations did you experience in relation to the event where you kept your agreement, versus the situation above where you did not keep your agreement or commitment

iv.   List any projects you have started and not completed. Why have you not completed the project? Are there new agreements that you can make that will allow you to continue with the project, or do you need to drop this project in order to get back into integrity?

v.   Describe a time when you agreed to follow through on something and then failed to do so. Why did you make the agreement in the first place? What went wrong? Was there more of a breach of integrity when you made the agreement or is the greater breach of integrity that you have not followed through?

vi.   Keep in mind that we may have some cleanup to do with respect to the commitments and agreements we have made thus far in our lives. As we go through a personal assessment of our beliefs and values, and we challenge ourselves on how we came to acquire and hold our existing beliefs and values, we may need to make some changes and offer some apologies.

Chapter 10.

Balanced Conversations

To authentically listen, we need to be comfortable with silence. During a conversation, people are often listening for an opportunity to interject and to add to the conversation. Often this prevents them from fully receiving the message being spoken to them. When it comes to being present and connected and listening authentically, one of the most difficult things to master is knowing when to interrupt or interject.

How long do you wait for someone to finish speaking if you truly want to hear everything they have to say and don't want to interrupt their thought process as they deliver their message? The best answer for someone who really needs to manage their listening practice is that the longer the better. Chances are, if you don't interrupt or interject when they expect you to, they will ask you for input and that's your cue to speak.

As a starting point, practice waiting at least 5 seconds before responding. It will feel like an eternity, and it will be transformative. You will learn a lot about others and yourself, and this listening practice will allow you to gain information and perspective beyond your wildest imagination.

There are people who at times may not have the capacity to maintain balance in a conversation. Sometimes a person may truly need to be heard and to clear some space from their mind. This release may show up as verbal diarrhea. This is the conversation where a person goes from topic to topic, stating one thought after another without allowing anyone to respond or interject.

This can be very frustrating for the listener. The listener may initially feel the need to add clarification or ask for additional insight. At some point, the listener may simply feel like their input is not wanted or appreciated. A speaker may do this if they are excited, nervous, or is simply worried they will forget what it is they need to share. And anyone going through a stressful time without a great support network may show up in this manner.

How does one respond appropriately in this situation? The first thing to note is that it is important to have compassion. The person venting is going through something. They are 'full' – they may be full of information, full of emotion, or simply lonely and in need of being listened to. When you want to try to interject, it's important to initially send non-verbal cues that you want to interject. You may, at some point, feel the need to verbally interrupt the speaker. The important thing is that when you do, you need to gauge the reaction.

If the speaker has a very strong need to vent and release, they may be unable or unwilling to listen or exchange with you anyway. In that case, keep listening, do your best to remember the most important details, and do your best to respond and give or request clarification when you do get the opportunity. Only if you truly listen will the speaker truly get to release enough that they can start to receive new information from you.

The Screaming Match - "You Are Not Listening to Me!!!"

Have you ever been in a conversation where both participants are accusing each other of not listening? Here is the first fact relating to this situation. When two people are in a conversation and one says, "You are not listening to me.", and the other replies, "YOU are not listening to ME!", I can guarantee neither person is being listened to effectively. Both are guilty of not listening to the other. I think this is becoming more and more common, and it absolutely indicates a severe communication breakdown.

Stress is a major factor in these situations, and emotions are intertwined within the messaging. In this situation, both participants are stuffed full of information, are emotionally attached to being listened to, and both need to release or vent. If neither one allows the other to release, they often end up screaming at one another. Since neither has the capacity to take in more information in the moment, they end up talking over one another. The volume of their voices becomes increasingly louder as each of them tries to force their message to be heard by the other. This is a very emotional encounter and may escalate to physical violence if neither party chooses to become the listener.

If you ever find yourself in this situation, before you lose your temper, just stop talking and start nodding because the other person simply cannot hear you anyway. This is especially difficult to do during a stressful situation where there may be a perceived shortage of time to complete the conversation as this creates a sense of urgency, and our natural tendency to *fight or flight* takes over. As much as you may feel a sense of urgency to complete the communication as soon as possible, the longer it takes you to realize that you must let the other person fully vent before they will have the capacity to listen to you, the longer it will take for you to successfully deliver your message.

If you can just find a way to stop talking, even if you don't yet have the capacity to listen fully to them, hopefully, you will listen well enough that they will clear out enough space to allow you to respond. The sooner you recognize this situation and stop talking, the sooner the other person will vent out, and the greater will be the opportunity to successfully complete the exchange of information.

If this is a work situation, and you were not able to successfully complete the interaction to the satisfaction of both parties, you may want to seek help from human resources or from a coworker or supervisor. If it is a personal situation, you may need to seek some assistance from a counselor, friend, or family member – I recommend someone neutral to the topic that will not take sides.

If you ever find yourself as a third-party observing others engaged in this type of heated exchange, you may want to attempt some form of pattern interrupt and see if you can get them both to take a break. Perhaps district one of them stating that you need their help urgently and just take them out of the situation for a few minutes. You might want to intervene and mediate, offering that each will get the opportunity to say everything they need to say, and you will listen to both. Because you will be able to listen more fully than either of them, you will more effectively allow them both to release.

The Seemingly Unengaged Conversation

There are people who at times simply do not seem to have a lot to add to the conversation. This may be an indication that there is a lack of connection, or this may occur if the person you are communicating with is simply taking in the information, considering it, and perhaps giving non-verbal feedback. If you are accountable for being present and connected, chances are, you will be able to correctly interpret the receiver's response, even if verbalization is minimal. You can also ask for confirmation of their understanding. If you are still left unsure, request a follow-up meeting, or consider following up in writing.

In business, and especially for salespeople, silence can be a great tool for uncovering information that the other party may have been withholding. Because people are so uncomfortable with silence, this practice can be a tool to cause the other party in a negotiation to provide you with important information or perhaps to 'show their hand.'

Exercise 13 – Practicing The 5-Second Rule

i.   On the phone – the next time you are on a phone call and the other person is speaking, and there is a break in their speaking, count to 5 on your fingers (one Mississippi, two Mississippi, three Mississippi, four Mississippi, five Mississippi)

ii. Then, if they have not started speaking again, you can respond. But if they start speaking, the exercise starts over!

iii. Because you will be placing some focus on waiting to respond, this does mean you will not truly be authentically and completely listening; you will be developing the most important tool in your toolbox of communication skills. The ability to remain silent and to be comfortable with silence is a very powerful communication tool.

iv. Journal about the experience. Note how it felt to wait this long before responding. How did the person you were conversing with respond to your delayed responses? Did you still get to say everything you needed to say by the end of the conversation? Were there things you realized you did not really need to say? Did the other person, at times, start speaking on a new topic just to break the silence?

v. Perform this same exercise the next time you are in a group meeting. The only exception is that if someone directly asks you a question, then you may respond as you normally would.

vi. Once you have gained some prowess, try this in a business setting.

Defining Responsibility in Conversation

In a conversation, whose job is it to ensure the message is communicated effectively - the speaker or the listener? The answer is "I". I must take responsibility as both listener and speaker or as presenter and audience. If I want to experience effective, efficient, and meaningful communication, then I must always be responsible in any situation or circumstance. There are no excuses. There is no one else to blame. If I am speaking, I need to find a way to ensure that the listener is truly understanding the message I am relating. If I am listening, I need to find a way to ensure I am receiving the message correctly. If I am accountable and responsible for any communication that I am party to, then there will be a much greater opportunity for success.

I am not saying that if we listen effectively there will never be a miscommunication event. Remember, we each have our own set of beliefs and filters that will determine how we interpret and receive a particular message. Our success as communicators is directly related to our level of conscious awareness and our level of accountability and commitment to communicating effectively and authentically as both giver and receiver.

Speaking Directly vs. Speaking in Inference

We have all met people who are very direct in their communications. They sometimes come across as cold, tactless, or ruthless. At these times, we may find ourselves saying, "At least we know where we stand." These direct speakers are the people that say exactly what they feel needs to be said in a very matter-of-fact tone, and they do not beat around the bush or sugarcoat anything.

Although this may seem cold, it also assumes that the listener is able to comprehend the message and deal with it physically, emotionally, intellectually, and spiritually. It assumes that the recipient can 'handle the truth', and when interpreted in this way, direct communication can be very effective for business.

In contrast, speaking in inference and 'beating around the bush' forces the listener to question – perhaps on a subconscious level – what the speaker is really trying to say. The receiver may wonder, "What is their point?" or "Why can't they just be more honest?" Speaking in inference can be 'tactful' and can be, at times, placating, but it can also come across as dishonest or manipulative. On the other hand, speaking in inference can also be very descriptive and metaphorical. It can produce colorful imagery that can be very engaging and interesting.

Listeners can also either listen directly or listen through inference. When a speaker speaks directly and the listener listens directly, communication can be very efficient. This can be optimal for business. But if the speaker speaks in inference, and the listener listens directly (takes the message literally), this is where the listener may perceive a lack of honesty or at the very least, will find the message unclear.

If a listener listens in inference, and the speaker speaks in inference, there will be a lot of interpretation occurring, and miscommunication will be common. If the listener listens in inference and the speaker is direct, the listener may feel like the speaker is being rude or tactless.

Becoming aware of our own and other's speaking and listening from the perspective of direct or inferential can help us look for potential breakdowns in communication. This is not the easiest concept to grasp, and there is no right or wrong. It is just a matter of becoming aware of this concept and the role it can play in communication and potential breakdowns or upsets. I do not intend to judge either direct or inferred speaking or listening as good or bad. It is just worth considering, as it may help one gain a new perspective in the light of potential communication breakdowns.

Communication also breaks down when one is not sensitive to other people's emotional triggers. Each of us has different levels of understanding and interest in different areas of our lives. Again, this relates back to factors such as one's religious or cultural beliefs, as well as someone's individual life experiences. By being truly present and aware, and by being in that Zen space where you can be in communication and observe the interaction at the same time, you will be able to recognize when a certain topic may be an area of pain or sensitivity for someone else.

We each also have different levels of awareness and the ability to remain balanced and focused. Due to the human nature of needing to 'be right' and 'look good', if we are not sensitive to another's responses or reactions, the possibility of making another person feel bad, look bad, or 'be made wrong' strongly exists. When we leave someone looking bad or we 'make them wrong' and leave them there, we truly make ourselves look bad. How we leave someone is a reflection back on us as a communicator.

By remaining balanced and aware, we increase our potential to create effective communication where everyone feels respected and dignified throughout the conversation. A truly responsible communicator pays attention to where they leave the people they engage in communication with. A true leader will always demonstrate respect and treat others with compassion and dignity.

How Learning Affects Listening

One key point about learning and listening relates to the number one enemy of learning… "I already know______." Already knowing is the greatest barrier to learning and is one of the greatest reasons why a listener stops listening. How often have you been in a conversation and been cut off by someone saying, "I already know what you are about to say, and______." And how often do you find yourself responding with, "Actually, I was going to say______."

Sometimes people are on the same wavelength, and they really can complete each other's sentences. Other times, the listener only thinks they are. The more open we are to learning, the less our 'already knowing' will cause us to become impatient and interrupt. Even if you really do *'already know"*, by listening attentively, you will allow the speaker to gain additional clarity themselves. Sometimes it helps increase understanding and clarifies interpretation for all parties in the communication when the speaker is given the space to repeat some 'already known' information.

While we might want to be efficient with our time by limiting repetition, if someone is consistently not listening due to a perception of already knowing, the result can be less efficient conversation, miscommunication, the need for further explanation and even upset. It is faster and takes less energy to transfer a message to an open receiver than to have to fight to deliver the message. Thus, by being open to authentically receiving repeated information, you may actually shorten the total length of the communication.

Persistent Problems

When there is an issue that will not go away for someone, they are most likely avoiding dealing with the issue. It may be that the issue is attached to some very complex and intense emotions. It may be a thought, an interaction with someone else, or some event or consideration that is 'nagging' at them. It could be related to difficulty at work, or they may be dealing with an illness, or perhaps they are experiencing a breakdown in a relationship at home.

Regardless of the cause of the persistent issue, until they allow themselves to deal with it and experience their feelings and emotions about the issue, they will have difficulty moving past it. Mental health challenges are becoming increasingly common, and suicide rates are on the rise. It is important to find a way to deal with any issues that we are stuffing down deep inside ourselves.

I remember checking Facebook at 2:30a.m. one year around Christmas time. I don't remember the exact message, but I saw a post from a friend that made me feel a chill down my spine. I could tell he was in a very dark place emotionally. I noted that the post had only been created about 15 minutes before, so I sent him a text and asked if he wanted to go for coffee. He said, "Yes." We ended up talking for a few hours. I found out his wife had cheated and was leaving him for the other man, and he was devastated. They had a daughter, and I convinced him to focus on his relationship with the child. It turned out he had called the police on himself earlier that day and had been contemplating suicide. I informed him that next time he had any suicidal thoughts, he should get himself to the nearest emergency room.

He was at such a dark place in that moment that he had considered ending his life. And because the universe gave me insomnia and nudged me to check Facebook, I found out he needed some help. I tell both friends and acquaintances when they are going through something, that I am that person who truly is okay with being called to go for coffee at 2:30 a.m. I will not hesitate. That night is one of the greatest experiences of my life, because I was able to be there for someone else. Although I would never want anyone to need me like that again, I will always welcome the opportunity to be there for the person that does need me.

Difficult People Are a Mirror

People who appear difficult are often just a reflection of what we are experiencing ourselves. The person is who they are, and we find them difficult to deal with in that moment. If we are experiencing them as difficult or rude, that is really our own internal issue. We are placing a judgment upon them, rather than just listening to where they are coming from. The opportunity exists to become present and listen to what they are saying. What is the volume, context, and intensity of their words? What non-verbal cues are being shared? Rather than being triggered by their foul mood, what can we discern about how they got into this mood? What is the message they are intending to communicate? What do they need?

Depending on our level of balance at the time of the interaction, a person may show up for us as angry or upset. In being responsible for the communication, we can choose to center, become present, and allow them to vent. We can respond in awe and wonder in response to how they show up for us. We can allow the other to experience their feelings and emotions by being present with them, avoiding any temptation to judge, and by authentically listening. By doing so we help them to deal with their issues and process their feelings. This gives us the power to affect the outcome of the interaction, and we can initiate a shift in the mood of the seemingly difficult person.

For me, there is no greater feeling than the feeling I get when I successfully facilitate the transformation of someone from being overtly hostile, to being cheerful and enthusiastic. It's an opportunity to bring gratitude and joy to them and to myself. I will never forget the first time I was on the receiving end of this – I walked into a branch of the CIBC bank in Toronto, Canada. I don't know what I was upset about, and it truly did not matter. I was in a horrible mood, and an angel of a bank teller – a woman in her 40's or 50's with short blonde hair and a beautiful smile listened to me, and then responded to me in a way that changed my attitude in an instant.

That bank teller was a customer service master! She could have made me feel wrong for being rude and for taking my frustrations out on her. But instead, she transformed my mood, and made my day, and it had nothing to do with solving the problem I had shown up at the bank to take care of. It was purely an energetic shift, that resulted from her allowing me to be as I was in that moment, and by listening to me without being attached to what or how I was speaking, or the outcome I was demanding. This is the power of engaging in authentic, present listening, and it is transformative for both the listener and the speaker.

Turning Anger into Enthusiasm

The following list of steps is designed to provide a process that will allow anyone willing to alter the mood of someone that is upset.

i. Physically Balance – you need to be balanced yourself to avoid being triggered by the other person. They may throw some curve balls at you, and although you may momentarily be thrown off balance emotionally, by intentionally balancing yourself prior to the interaction, you should be able to recover immediately if thrown off.

ii. Remember - "I am not the reason this person is upset, and I care enough to find out what caused this upset". Put yourself in their shoes and do your best to listen without judgment to their perspective.

iii. Reassure – remind them that you want to help and ask for their perspective.

iv. Remove any physical barriers to communication.

v. Acknowledge the person's upset or frustration (you do not have to state agreement, but rather simply acknowledge where they are coming from.) If you are concerned that they may become aggressive, again reassure them that you are there to help and ask that they please assist you in helping them by as calmly as possible sharing what has occurred for them. It may also help to use a tone that is closer to their tone, but just a little calmer. If you speak to them in a tone that is too much quieter than theirs, they may not pay attention, and if you come in louder, you may cause an escalation in their anger.

vi. Listen authentically. Give them your full attention. Do not cut them off, as they must be able to vent until they are truly complete. While they are speaking, acknowledge that you are listening with a nod, or "u-huh", etc. Wait a second or two after they stop talking, and say, "I got that," or "O.K.". Ask for clarification on anything if needed. If you truly listen to the cause of their upset, you will build their trust, and then they may be willing to move on to resolution. If you argue, they will escalate.

vii.   Offer a solution. If you cannot do what they are asking, you can state that you fully comprehend their perspective and can appreciate why they are upset. Then offer a solution. If you cannot provide the solution they desire, you can apologize for not having the authority to do so. Then you must repeat what you are able to offer them. Stay focused on what is possible, rather than getting locked into an argument about what is not possible.

viii.   Direct the conversation away from the cause of the upset, and toward the possibilities for resolution. Note that 10-20% of the entire conversation should be about the problem, and 80-90% of the discussion should focus on resolution.

Shifting Moods at Work

In any business, if you need something from someone - perhaps your boss or a coworker – but that person is in a bad mood, you may want to help shift their mood in preparing them to receive your request. I used to have a boss that tended to appear to me as overtly hostile. Whether in person or on the phone, I would quickly gauge his mood. If I felt he was in a bad mood, I would ask an open-ended question such as, "How are things going today?" It did not matter that the obvious answer was horrible. Just ask the question and wait until they open the floodgates. He would start venting, and I would sincerely listen and acknowledge. I was allowing him to process whatever had been happening that upset him. He would take about 10 minutes to complete his venting - and in doing so, he would resolve the issue for himself and determine his next steps.

Once he had cleared that space, he would ask why I called, and I would then make my request. I usually got what I asked for, and my sales went through the roof. I became one of the top two performers in the country, and my exceptional sales numbers over four consecutive years of working with that manager allowed me to get multiple job offers in California. I was then able to achieve my teenage dream of moving to live near the beach in Southern California, where I remain to this day.

From Hostile to Loyal

Most people steer clear of anyone who raises their voice or appears angry or hostile. They judge the behavior as inappropriate and try to distance themselves from the person who is angry. This is often done out of concern for one's own safety, and that may be a good choice in certain situations. Each person needs to decide for themselves, and I recommend paying close attention to one's instincts in tense situations.

We generally think of overt hostility as the most negative emotion, and cheerful expression of enthusiasm as an extremely positive emotion. But what about apathy? What about Altruism? Consider the saying, "It's the quiet ones that will surprise you." Where did that saying come from? I searched the internet for the source of that saying, and it is so commonly used that my search for the original source was to no avail.

The real extremes of emotion are altruism and apathy. Calm and optimistic enthusiasm is a fair definition of altruism, and altruism is generally accepted as the highest state of conscious being – this is the self-actualized individual. Apathy tends to show up as silent sadness. The apathetic person is void of hope and is quietly giving up on life. They have no fight left in them. This is the opposite of altruism, and therefore I see altruism and apathy as being the true extremes of emotion.

The Monster Within

Overt hostility may be a lower level of consciousness than cheerful enthusiasm, and we can get almost unanimous agreement that it's a lot more fun to be around someone who is cheerful and enthusiastic. These smiling, happy people attract us with their charisma, and their laughter is contagious.

Now here's the rub — both overt hostility and cheerful enthusiasm come from a place of passion, caring and commitment. These are the people that take action and produce results. They are in the mid-range of emotions, not the extremes. As such, someone who appears hostile or angry can easily be moved to cheerful and enthusiastic. It's a matter of dissolving their considerations through the process of present listening. This is a much more altruistic and powerful response than making them feel wrong for their behavior in the moment.

For situations where you are not in any physical danger, if you can engage someone who is overtly hostile or angry and dissolve their considerations, their anger may be transformed into enthusiasm, and they will become very loyal to you. Why do they become loyal? People appreciate being authentically listened to, and on a subconscious level, it feels great to clear space!

As a result of the interaction, the previously hostile person will feel good, and this will cause them to experience gratitude towards you. Even if you were not able to give them what they thought they wanted in that exchange, they received something much more valuable from you – you allowed them to experience their emotions and clear their upset in a safe space of non- judgment. They now respect and appreciate you for your humanity and for validating their experience.

This reminds me of one of my favorite books, "Have You Hugged a Monster Today?" by Alen Cohen. It's a great book to keep in the bathroom or on the coffee table. It's a short and inspiring read. I have been a monster. I have also hugged a monster. It's about being passionate and demonstrating compassion for others. When we are triggered by an apparent monster, sometimes it's just that we are reminded of the monster that lives within each of us.

Chapter 11.

More Powerful Acts of Communication

In this chapter you are being given a series of additional communication tools and concepts that can be useful in a variety of situations. Although some may seem obvious, the details and innuendos associated can make a huge difference in their effectiveness. This chapter will help you to utilize them wisely and effectively.

Questions, Statements and Declarations

Questions are used to request or elicit information. Statements are generally utilized to provide information. A declaration is a statement that is interpreted as being very assertive.

Assertions vs. Assessments

Assertions and assessments are generally both considered statements. An assessment is a statement of opinion but generally is not easily supported by facts or by objective information. Assessments are purely subjective. Assessments may or may not be true, and they are hard to prove. The most common type of proof for an assessment is the agreement of others. If others hold the same opinion, that agreement can lend weight to the information and can give the perception of authority to the person making the assessment.

Assessments are ungrounded if no statements of objective supporting information are offered to support the assessment. Assessments can be grounded by offering assertions that consist of objective and verifiable information. Assertions are also statements, and they are a little easier to prove or disprove, as they can always be verified with objective data.

Not all verifiable information is true and correct, and sometimes what one thinks is a scientific fact today can be proven incorrect at some point in the future. But an assertion can always be measured and verified. The statement, "It was hotter than hell," is subjective and therefore is an assessment. The statement, "It was 80 degrees Celsius," is an assertion. It is possible to verify the temperature. It could also be proven at some point that the thermometer was incorrect and needed to be calibrated, but it is still possible to verify the statement, making it an assertion. If you follow the assessment with the statement that it was 80 degrees, the assessment becomes somewhat grounded. Now we can question how 80 degrees Celsius compares to the temperature in hell. I suspect hell is significantly hotter than 80 degrees Celsius, but I don't know if there is any scientific data to prove that.

Sometimes a speaker delivering a message may deliver an assessment from the belief that their assessment is true or factual. This is a common source of communication breakdown. The speaker may lose credibility if the audience or listener questions the validity of the assessment. A listener may seek assertions or factual evidence to prove or disprove the speaker's opinion. Any time a speaker states an opinion as though it is fact unless the listener is in complete agreement, the message spoken will likely be met with doubt and be questioned for its validity.

Certain facts that are backed up by experts and are accepted as true today might be disproved by another expert at some point in the future. Although we have some scientific laws and fact-based information that are generally accepted on a global level by respected experts, the beauty of our world is that we have so much more to explore and learn. No matter how factual something might seem today, there is always the possibility that it will be disproven tomorrow. With this understanding, we can allow ourselves to respond in wonder and awe – as opposed to judgment – when presented with information that conflicts with our currently held beliefs.

Requests, Offers and Promises

Requests are things we ask others to do for us. Offers are things we propose that we could do for someone else. And a promise is our word. When we make a promise, we make a commitment. Real commitments are attached to specific conditions of satisfaction and a set timeline for completion.

In business, when we need to get things done efficiently and effectively, communication must involve offers, requests, and commitments. If there is a meeting or a discussion, and statements are made – regardless as to whether those statements were declarations, assessments, assertions, or questions – if no offers or requests are made, then the communication is nothing more than gossip.

For business to move forward, offers and requests must be made, and for business to move forward efficiently, there must be commitments that include detailed roles and responsibilities assigned, timelines detailed, and conditions of satisfaction agreed upon. Business plans and sales plans are based on the aforementioned information and include supporting objective and subjective evidence to support the validity of the plan.

Complaints

Complaints are a part of daily life and are needed to communicate concerns, considerations, and expectations. For some people, their past has been filled with complaints and criticisms that were delivered in a way that was demeaning, disrespectful or degrading. As a result, many of us avoid confrontation and choose to be 'tactful' or perhaps even downright dishonest to avoid having to provide a critique or engage in a confrontation.

Some people don't complain until they pass the breaking point and lose their temper, and others keep everything bottled up inside till the day they die. Conditions of satisfaction cannot be met if we don't speak up when there are issues. It is important to see criticism and complaints as valuable tools to communicate and confirm our expectations and how well they are being met.

If we are speaking to an employee and coming from the perspective of a coach wanting to help an employee improve performance, the communication can be very productive and will often transfer a sense of confidence to the employee as they are included in laying out a plan of action. Appropriate communication will let the employee know what they need to do to meet the conditions of satisfaction and get a good performance review in the future.

A contractor who is doing their job may believe that everything is going spectacularly, while you may not feel the same way. In this situation, if you fail to complain and make a request for change, you exceed your expectations. By respectfully sharing your complaint and being open to conversation about the work, it becomes much more likely that the contractor and customer will end up with a shared vision for the project. When the client makes a complaint, the contractor is given the opportunity to change course and meet the conditions of satisfaction, resulting in an outcome that everyone will appreciate. The key is to be centered and aware prior to making a complaint and to deliver the complaint respectfully while ensuring everyone's dignity is kept whole.

When giving a complaint or a criticism, we need to hold and view the other person as able. In a relationship, sometimes a person will hold off ending the relationship due to fear of hurting their partner's feelings. If, in their own mind, the relationship is over, the person desiring the breakup may just start seeing other people without firs communicating the desire to break up. This is a complete disrespect to their partner, and the fear of hurting their partner's feelings was used as an excuse to cheat. Everyone would be better off with respect, honesty, and dignity. There may be some pain felt in the moment, but that pain will only be delayed and worsened by withholding the truth and delaying the inevitable.

In a work situation, if a manager does not believe an employee is able, they may simply take action to fire the employee rather than discuss the role and how the employee can improve. This can result in high turnover rates as well as lost talent. Often, the replacement will then fall short in different areas rather than be an overall better employee. Sometimes we don't know what we have until we have lost it, and the best way to prevent that scenario is to communicate more effectively.

If there is a situation where you have good reason to feel that your assessment of a situation or another person is grounded, and you are uncomfortable having a conversation with them about it, you may need to consider involving another party in a meeting or mediation. Whenever it is possible to hold and view the other person as being able, the recipient will feel that you have confidence in them, and they will feel your confidence as a potential for a positive outcome.

Please note that if you are uncomfortable with the conversation and you delay the conversation because of your own discomfort, it is you who are allowing the issue to fester. It is you that are not able to handle the situation. In fact, the other party might not even be aware that an issue exists at all.

Compliments

A compliment is very similar to a criticism, although usually more pleasant to give and receive. People are usually more confident giving compliments than criticisms. However, many people are insecure about receiving compliments. Depending on one's beliefs, and social or personal history, compliments may at times cause the receiver to be very uncomfortable. The receiving of a compliment is also affected by a listener that listens with inference, or a compliment given by someone who tends to speak through inference, as inferences can raise the question of motive.

The best way to give a compliment is to be specific and direct. For example, "You look great today" leaves a lot of room for inference and might come across as less sincere than a more detailed and direct compliment. "You look great today. That blue shirt is stylish, and it compliments your complexion" comes across as much more authentic.

In a corporate setting, some compliments may be on the verge of breaking human resource policies. Therefore, at work, it is much safer to compliment others on their job performance only. "Jack, that was a great report you presented to the operations team. It was very detailed and gave clear, objective data in support of your recommendations."

Understanding The Perpetration Cycle

A perpetrator is one who commits an unlawful or dishonest act that affects another. When we are dishonest or withhold key information from another in a way that may ultimately be to protect our own ego or hide our mistakes, we initiate the perpetration cycle. Remember this phrase by Sir Walter Scott from 1808, "*Oh, what a tangled web we weave, when first we practice to deceive.*" When we lay down that first lie, we set in motion a string of lies that will continue to worsen the problem.

In business, when an employee tries to cover a mistake, or withholds important information, they can ultimately cost the company thousands or even millions of dollars, and the domino of additional problems may occur as a result. It may result in breakdowns in communication and bad decisions that can have very far-reaching effects. They can ruin careers for the perpetrator or victims of the perpetration. The collateral damage can cause low morale, and divisiveness amongst co-workers and teams and may result in damages that affect clients and customers.

The Impact of Stress

The more stress a person is experiencing, the more difficult it becomes to return to center, and to make good decisions. According to the Mayo Clinic, as published on the Mayo Clinic website, people under stress are more likely to experience anxiety and depression, mental health breakdowns, and physical health challenges. Stress causes the release of adrenaline and the 'stress hormone' cortisol. With these hormones, heart rate and blood pressure are increased, allowing the person to temporarily become stronger, faster, and more reactive. Normally, this is a temporary state known as the 'fight or flight' response, and it lasts for mere seconds or, at the most, a few minutes.

Although this may sound great to an athlete in training, there are some negative long-term side effects to having elevated levels of adrenaline and cortisol coursing through your veins. When a person is under unrelenting stress – perhaps due to multiple issues in their lives such as tension at work, problems in their marriage, or a loved one with health issues – this prolonged stress causes the fight or flight reaction to remain turned on.

Cortisol suppresses digestion, and changes how the immune system functions. With the stress reaction prolonged, increased heart rate and blood pressure, limited digestion, altered immune responses, multiple unwanted mental and physical health manifestations may occur.

Imagine the impact that stress will have not just on communication but on an employee's overall job performance. Anything that can be done to ensure employees are not under excessive stress at work, and to offer support and counselling if there are personal issues affecting the employee, will serve to support both the employee and the organization in the long run.

The Power of Apology

There is probably no greater tool in communication than an apology. At the same time, most people do not know how to deliver an apology. Usually, people confuse an apology with the words, "I am sorry." "I am sorry" is a statement about how the person delivering the apology feels inside. The words "I am sorry" often feel insincere to the recipient, and this is because the focus remains on the feelings and emotions of the speaker making the apology and not on the recipient of the apology.

For an apology to be effective, it needs to be declared as an offering. The person offering an apology must be centered and authentic, and they must clearly declare what it is they are apologizing for. The best way to improve the authenticity of an apology is to include as much detail as possible. It is also perfectly acceptable to apologize on behalf of someone else or on behalf of your company.

Even if you were not the one who wronged the other, you can still be responsible and accountable in the moment and offer an apology. Even if you are not able to fix the problem, you can still apologize for the circumstances despite them being beyond your control. Not every apology is perfect, and despite that, they are almost always appreciated. And even if you are unable to cure the situation, it is still commendable that you owned up to being responsible and accountable.

Owning up to Mistakes

Owning up to a mistake might feel very uncomfortable in the moment, but it is truly a position of power. There is power in knowing that you were the cause of the matter, as that admission opens the possibility to prevent future mistakes.

When mistakes are hidden or blamed on external circumstances, there is no opportunity to learn from the mistake. Often in a business, when an employee makes a mistake, and in particular a repeated mistake, it can reveal a problem with a system or a need for professional development.

When there is a culture in the work environment that allows mistakes to be viewed with wonderment and analysis rather than judgment and punishment, the organization and its people will grow from each situation.

Chapter 12.

Building Rapport

Most businesses have revenue that depends on relationships with other people. The ability to build rapport is crucial to strategic partnerships, building clientele, and motivating employees. The most effective form of advertising is word-of-mouth, and the easiest form of revenue is a return customer. Thus, it is extremely important that we build strong rapport with everyone with whom we interact. Even in the most hierarchical of structures, the quality and efficiency of the work performed by an employee will be better and faster if you have a strong rapport.

The following are some key steps that will lead to the development of excellent rapport:

i. Be centered and aware - This is the basis of communication and the basis of building rapport.

ii. Be authentic - This may mean smiling, but don't force it if it would not be authentic in the moment.

iii. Consistently greet and acknowledge people - This makes them feel important. Everyone should feel important. If someone in your organization is not important, why are they there? Everyone's contribution to a business is important.

iv.   Make appropriate eye contact - If you make eye contact with someone, and they look away with discomfort, then you also should look away for a moment and then re-connect. Be sensitive to the comfort level of others, and then gradually help them to feel more comfortable. Some cultures do not value eye contact, and some have laws against it, so mirroring the reaction of the other may be especially helpful in a multi-cultural environment.

v.   Humanity must come first - Care about others, and not just those you need something from. Have compassion for everyone and treat all with dignity. In the Introduction of this book, I referred to a book written in 1987 by Tom Peters. Tom's newest book – published in 2021 – is entitled "Excellence Now: Extreme Humanism," and highlights the moral responsibility of the enterprise, and requests that every leader for the good of the company, community, customer, and planet puts people first.

vi.   Listen for qualities of verbal communication – Receiving verbal communication is more than words. Verbal communication includes tone, pitch, speed, volume, clarity, and pacing.

vii.   Written communication - One of the greatest differences between verbal messages and written messages is the lack of intonation. Punctuation can help, and apps with emojis also provide additional information about the message. When a message is read from an email or text, the energy and qualities that were in the mind of the writer of the message are frequently lost on the receiver.

viii.   Context may help. The use of capital letters tends to indicate yelling so if you don't want to yell in an email or text, make sure you don't have your keyboard set for 'All Caps". If you are trying to communicate emotion, you are going to have to be creative. Find ways to communicate your emotions with parentheses, capitals, emojis and punctuation or by adding photos, videos, or gifs.

ix.   Be aware of non-verbal cues – Most messaging comes through non-verbal communication. Non-verbal communication may provide context, or it may be the entire message. Non-verbal communication includes eye contact, posture, touch, space, gestures, movement, and expression. Use your senses and harness your intuition to receive both verbal and non-verbal cues.

x.   Be respectful – You get what you give, so being respectful of others is the best way to receive respect from others.

xi.   Be true to yourself - The first 7 points focused on your ability to communicate authentically and to be attentive and respectful and compassionate toward others. But this does not mean at the expense of yourself. You must honor others and yourself at the same time.

xii.   Be honest and remain in integrity - It can take a lot of work to build trust, and one tiny mistake to lose it. Nothing expedites business relationships and the signing of contracts faster than a trusting relationship. And nothing puts the brakes on faster than suspicion. The smallest white lie can make others question you in future conversations, so be impeccable with your word.

Chapter 13.

Persuasion and Sales

Persuasion is the process by which we all endeavor to bring others to agree with or to adopt our own ideas and perspectives and to act on them. This chapter ties together persuasion, sales, and listening.

The main difference between persuasion and sales is that persuasion is not associated with the negative stereotypes that have been linked to sales professionals. There are times when we all need to 'sell' our ideas or get someone to 'buy-in' to our cause. Being persuasive is generally thought of as being less 'pushy' or less 'manipulative' than selling. Persuasion is rooted in the belief of the persuader about the value of the product, service, concept, or idea that one endeavors to get others to agree to. We all have ideas to sell every day – to our children, spouses, co-workers, managers, employees, etc. The need to be persuasive in our personal and professional lives is unavoidable and undeniable.

To be persuasive, we need to believe in what we are promoting, and we need to be relatable with the person or people to whom we are promoting. To avoid being perceived as pushy, manipulative, impatient, selfish, or annoying, we need to come from the belief that our product or service is beneficial for those we want to gain agreement from.

When we are centered, we will be more successful in presenting our ideas and receiving agreement. And when we are mindful, centered, and aware, we can observe ourselves as we present our offers and requests while also observing the responses of those to whom we are presenting. In this purposeful mindset, we will be able to respond, redirect, clarify and reposition as needed. And we will be capable of realizing if the receiver even needs what we are offering, or if we should suggest something different.

Perhaps we can offer something better or more appropriate. The stereotypical salesperson would simply continue to push their agenda, while the persuasive professional is able to receive and give simultaneously as they achieve the best possible outcome for all involved. Persuasive people possess the ability to reach others on a deeper subconscious level while having an emotional impact. They achieve this impact by going beyond determining superficial needs to understanding the associated implications of addressing those needs.

Disruptive Technology

To truly become successful in sales, one must master the ability to identify specific needs and then reveal the implications that meeting those needs - or failing to meet those needs - will have on several aspects of the prospective buyer's life. We need to help our clients and customers in their quest to help others and to enjoy a better quality of life. How will what we are offering affect the customer's customer - their employees, spouse, children, friends, etc.?

For example, I used to sell spine implants and would attend surgeries that lasted several hours. Surgery days were long, and I was trapped in the operating room until the surgeries were complete. One significant part of almost every spine surgery that added an hour to every operation was able to be replaced by a new technology… a new but extremely expensive product that meant less pain and faster healing for the patient.

This new technology shaved off so much time from the surgeries that the surgeons made more money per hour, and they could either do more surgeries per day or have more personal time. As a sales rep and single parent, I also made more money in less time and was able to be home with my child several hours earlier on surgery days. Additionally, the hospital was saving an estimated $800 per minute, which covered the cost of the very expensive new technology several times over. This is an example of a disruptive technology, and the implications went way beyond the initial consideration of less pain and faster healing for the patient.

At first glance, the cost of the new product was 3 to 4 times the cost of the current product. This was a line-item budget disaster and could have been a hard "no" for purchasing agents. But the implications for quality of life, added to hidden savings and potential revenue for everyone involved, resulted in a product where the objection to price was inconsequential.

Revealing Needs and Implications

Needs are easy to uncover with open-ended questions. An open-ended question cannot be answered with a 'yes' or a 'no'. The answer must be considered and created by the person answering. The implications of fulfilling one's needs are powerful in motivating customers to purchase and to follow through on utilizing the products and services effectively.

Open-ended questions stimulate the buyer to consider the needs and implications. The need for the technology mentioned above was to reduce pain and expedite healing time. For the doctor, the main needs were patient satisfaction and completing the surgery faster. The American hospital is a profit center and is generally averse to allowing new products that come with expensive price tags. They are watching, first and foremost, their profits and losses represented by line-item budgets. Because of the disruptive technology, the implications of meeting those needs were so far reaching that it was possible to get everyone involved to agree, but it was not as easy as a sale driven by offering a competitive price.

The key to uncovering needs and implications is to have the customer tell the persuasive sales professional what their needs and implications are before the buyer is even consciously aware of them. To really gain the buy-in of the customer, drawing out any emotions that are attached to the implications of meeting their needs are the emotional triggers that result in completed transactions. Rather than telling the customer what considerations they should have, we want to become masterful at utilizing questions and directing the conversation in such a way that the customer verbalizes them to us as they explore them in their own minds.

The persuasive professional will set the stage for the customer to think out loud and provide valuable information about their deepest subconscious needs and the associated implications that our product or service addresses. Having them reveal the impact on their lifestyle and the emotions that will come up as a result is crucial. In this way, we help them discover and review their own considerations as they tell us how we can successfully motivate them to take action.

The product I referred to in the example above was bone morphogenetic protein or BMP-2. The surgeon needed to perform a spinal fusion and desired to reduce the patient's pain, decrease the length of the surgery, and have the patient heal as fast as possible. The hospital and doctor would be rated by the insurance companies on the percentage of good vs. bad patient outcomes – such as what percentage of patients healed with no complications, with as little pain medication as possible, and how quickly they return to work and their activities of daily living. This technology sped up healing, caused a higher percentage of patients to recover faster, decreased the overall use of pain medication, and allowed patients to return to work faster.

Eliminating patients' pain faster is a highly emotional positive outcome. Surgeons getting home to their families earlier and spending quality time with their children is a highly emotionally positive outcome. For the hospital executives marketing the emotional outcomes of faster healing, less pain and faster return to the activities of daily living meant increased revenue and bonuses. Bonuses resulted in more vacations, awards, salary increases, and promotions. It is the basic need that is tied to greater implications that are attached to emotional outcomes that ultimately trigger the decision to complete the transaction for an expensive but disruptive technology.

5 Seconds of Silence as a Sales Tool

Being mindful, centered, and aware; and managing our own belief while we ask open-ended questions to stimulate the thought process of our customer allows us to guide the customer to talk themselves into making the purchase. When we apply 5 seconds of silence in receiving answers being communicated to us, we allow much more information to flow from the end user and buyer. And as we practice present listening, we can receive and process all the information that flows out. We want to listen to what the customer says, even if it is not what we had anticipated. A professional salesperson plans their sales call and has anticipated the customer's responses to their presentation. They may be listening for keywords and phrases or cues to jump in with their response to the customer's anticipated objections. This planning can be beneficial if the salesperson focuses on listening to what is being communicated.

However, listening for pre-planned objections or answers, and attempting to drive in planned pitches, may cause the salesperson to be deaf to the customer's rationale for choosing to purchase. Sales artistry involves creating the space and influencing the conversation that leads the customer talking themselves into saying "Yes."

Speaking Directly INTO the Customer's Listening

The salesperson that appears pushy or manipulative is stuffing the potential customer with information that the customer is not ready to receive. The present listener that sets the conversation in motion with appropriate open-ended questions is clearing space for the prospective buyer to think about all the needs and implications they may experience. Listening and being silent while the buyer processes their response and then communicates it, allows the salesperson to appropriately interject with new and valuable information, and to do so while speaking into the buyer's listening.

When you are speaking directly into the customer's listening, you have listened so carefully to the buyer, that not only did you receive their spoken message, but you also became aware of how they are listening to you. You have taken note of the filters through which they are listening and speaking and are now able to speak in a way - that even after they filter your message - they will receive that message in the way you intended. This allows you to connect much more deeply with your customer, and what you offer will truly meet their needs. This is the power of empowered communication. If the product or service is truly beneficial for the prospect, they will usually talk themselves into buying when provided this type of opportunity to do so.

Chapter 14.

Responding to a Speaker

Imagine that you are in a conversation or listening to a presentation, and you are centered and aware. You are authentically listening to the message that is being presented. And now a thought comes to you, and you want to ask for clarification or add some information, or perhaps just express agreement. How do you do this if you are not supposed to interrupt?

Interruptions

What effect will the interruption have on the speaker and on other listeners? In the blink of an eye, you must determine the need vs. the implications of interrupting the speaker. If it's possible to make a mental note, or even a written note, and then save the thought, do that. What is the purpose of the interruption? Do you need to clarify for the speaker, for yourself and/or other listeners? Do you have crucial additional information to provide? Is a correction needed? Do you need to express agreement and provide acknowledgement or perhaps pay a compliment?

Non-Verbal Cues

Only interrupt if you truly have a beneficial purpose that outweighs the implications of interrupting the speaker's flow. And if you must interrupt, try to do so with a non-verbal cue?

You might be able to communicate via expression, clapping, nodding or some other means rather than speaking. If it is necessary to interrupt, raise your hand, stand, or give some other physical cue to get the speaker's attention. Perhaps eye contact with a facial expression that you want to speak. Also observe the speaker's non-verbal response to your non-verbal interruption. When you gesture that you want to interrupt, does the speaker cue you to speak, or does the speaker cue you to wait? Again, reassess the necessity of the interruption.

Respect

Respecting others when they have the floor is very important. Always be as respectful as possible. Failing to be respectful may damage your own identity and credibility, and ensuring you have permission from the speaker to interrupt makes a huge impact on how you are received. Having been involved in organizing conferences and meetings, there have been times when I needed to interrupt a speaker for various reasons. Perhaps to alert them to a question from an audience member, to provide a note about a personal emergency, or to let them know their time was up and we need to move on to the next speaker.

In any situation, it is crucial to be respectful and to provide cues. Being consistent with cues is very helpful. For example, I developed the pattern of letting speakers know their time was up by positioning myself against the wall in line with the podium. As the meeting progressed from speaker to speaker, they would see me come up the aisle at the side of the room and gaze (not stare) in their direction. By the middle of the first day, the speakers knew to wrap up as soon as I go up from my seat to walk towards my position at the wall.

Planning Questions & Interruptions

During talks where questions were going to be allowed, we would let the audience know the process for asking questions prior to the commencement of that talk. When I did stand-up comedy, we would be given a pre-agreed verbal signal to indicate we had 30 seconds to wrap up. If you are organizing a meeting, or leading an event, consider creating and communicating a set of rules for interruptions or questions; and you may want to have questions submitted and reviewed in advance of the talk. Also, always leave room in the schedule to accommodate speakers going over their time limits. It is inevitable.

As a speaker, state your own preferences at the start of your talk. As a listener, if you truly need to interrupt even though the cues and your instincts are telling you the speaker won't appreciate it, ensure you have considered the consequences and that they truly are worth the negative impact of making an undesirable interruption.

Chapter 15.

Presenting with Slides

Most presenters put their entire talk on their slides. If you are utilizing the slides to build an e-learning module, that might work. But, if you are presenting to a group and want to be able to connect with the audience and have them engaged with you as a speaker, this is not a good idea. Your audience will be working on reading your presentation rather than listening. They will be in their own heads, reading and interpreting without listening to you. They may be hearing you, but they may not be present and listening.

Here are some key points to being a great presenter and utilizing slides to your full advantage:

i.   Know your material - You must know and fully understand the material you are presenting. You should be able to restate it in a variety of ways for listeners who might not understand your message the way you say it initially. If you notice there appears to be confusion or someone raises their hand with a question, you should know the material well enough to explain it to any listener. There can be an exception if these are unqualified listeners. In this case, you need to recognize that they may not have enough base knowledge on the topic to grasp the concept in that moment, and you can express to them that you will attempt to address their question after the presentation.

ii.   Consider the Purpose - Your slides have specific and limited purposes. First, they act as a prompt or an outline that you can follow to ensure you do not miss any of the information you intend to include in your presentation. Secondly, they can be utilized to provide context or to emphasize certain points. An effective slide will not be packed with words. Simply adding a photo, a video, or just some keywords or phrases can benefit both the speaker and the audience. Slides can also be used to provide contact information, credentials, and references or to add humor to the presentation.

iii.   Attractive and Easy to See - Slides need to be easy to see. Any text, photos, or graphics should be clear with contrast against the background color of the slide. Colors used on the slides should be attractive, without having the colors become overwhelming. You may want to further research the use of colors from psychological and/or marketing perspectives. just keep it simple and use as few words as possible in a large, easy-to-read font.

iv.   Using Notes - Have the bulk of your presentation fully integrated into your own mind. If you need to keep some notes for yourself, it is better to have those notes somewhere handy other than on your slideshow. I do like utilizing PowerPoint Notes to create notes that correspond with each specific slide. The pages with the notes can be printed and kept on the podium for easy reference during the presentation. Also, the process of creating notes pages at the same time as you create your presentation will help you remember the presentation better and decrease the need to refer to your notes while presenting.

v.   Interact With Your Audience - Finding ways to interact with your audience will keep them engaged with your presentation. Make eye contact! One audience member at a time, engage them in eye contact. Do NOT do this by going top to bottom, left to right, one audience member at a time in sequence. It is better to randomly move throughout the room… just make sure your cover the whole room, stopping randomly at one listener, and then another and another for at least 10 to 30 seconds each. If they know when it will be their turn to make eye contact, they will be able to disengage until you get close to them. And when you are making connection with one listener at a time, the energy of that connection will be felt by everyone. Too many presenters tend to look over everyone's heads and not really make eye contact with anyone. If you are engaging one audience member at a time and connecting with people from different areas of the audience, everyone in the audience will notice and feel that engagement, and that will cause them to remain alert.

vi.   Blind Eye Contact - For exceptionally large audiences – such as stadiums or large theatres - where there are lights in your eyes, and you cannot truly make eye contact, pick points where you know there are audience members and do your best to make eye contact with the audience one person at a time, as though you are able to look into each person's eyes. This is a way of energetically connecting with several specific audience members, even if you cannot truly see their eyes.

vii.   Have a microphone handy – you may want to allow the audience to ask questions or provide immediate commentary at some point during your presentation. This is often best left for the end of the presentation, but each speaker is different. Be creative! The better you know your material, the easier it will be to allow more questions and interruptions without being thrown off balance or losing track of time.

viii. Smile if appropriate. Use appropriate emotion and expression. And please do not just read your slides. Minimize the wordiness of your slides and have notes available. You will come across as much more knowledgeable by pausing to refer to a note than if the audience sees that you are simply reading your entire presentation to them from the slideshow.

ix. Share Your Enthusiasm – One of the key points of any presentation is to speak from your experience. In doing so, your passion and enthusiasm for the topic will be felt and experienced by the audience. Even dry scientific data can be delivered with passion and enthusiasm from the presenter's experience – especially if they manage their belief for the presentation. Speakers are chosen because of their experience and specific expertise, so share the information from your experience with your own passion and enthusiasm, and in doing so, you will inspire the audience. One of my best examples of this was my statistics professor in university. He was an ex-NHL hockey player with a dark sense of humor – usually relating to death statistics. When teaching, he would use examples that he himself found interesting or fun. I still remember some of his examples. I personally sucked at stats, but he remains one of my most memorable professors.

Chapter 16.

Summary

As a result of reading this book and embodying the concepts offered, you now have the tools to transform your communication, your business, and your personal successes. Beyond just learning how to communicate more effectively, you now have the tools to be a masterful and engaging leader. The more we remain mindful, balanced, aware, and capable of observing ourselves and others interacting, communicating, presenting, directing, performing, and producing, the better we will be at minimizing the gap between the vision we have of ourselves and the decisions we make that are not congruent with that vision. By being aware of our internal state, we are automatically more aware of our environment and our interactions and communications with others. With that awareness comes greater consciousness and a deeper understanding of our past motivations that led to the decisions and actions we chose. We will realize our past mistakes and may have some serious regrets, and we can see where we succeeded as well. As such, we can consciously decide to think, speak, and take actions in the present and the future that will produce our desired outcomes.

This entire book has been a guide to becoming an Empowered Communicator with the focus on being an engaged, authentic, compassionate listener. You have been provided with concepts and exercises that will allow you to continue to develop ongoing practices of mindfulness, centering and awareness that will lead to you and your teams becoming better and better at authentically listening and receiving information as intended. With a commitment to the ongoing practice of these techniques, you will produce exceptional results both professionally and personally.

This book has also demonstrated how to utilize these practices to be a successful leader, manager, business owner, sales professional, and humanitarian. We continue to be impacted by a major global crisis, for which the fallout is impacting us socially, economically, politically, and personally in virtually all aspects of our lives. We are facing drastic challenges in our businesses, and we are facing devastating crises of both physical and mental health. Socially, we have become polarized into the *we's* and *they's* of a variety of political, medical, and personal debates. These problems are cyclical. This is not the first time, nor will it be the last, that humanity will face a crisis of this magnitude.

The good news is that we will get through this crisis, as our ancestors have come through past global crises. In the meantime, as stated by business author Tom Peters in his 2021 book Excellence Now: Extreme Humanism "Humane and thoughtful and caring inclusive gestures toward our team members, our communities, and our customers must become our bread and butter and meat and potatoes." And "Excellence, by my [Tom Peters] definition, is first and foremost a way of life, a way of behaving with care and respect toward our fellow human beings and our communities day in and day out, moment in and moment out. Excellence is, in an important way, spiritual."

Having read this book, one might think, "Great. All I need to do is be mindful, balanced, and aware, and listen authentically." Although this may be true, what this book has done is helped you develop the tools to engage in the practice of mindfulness, returning to your center of balance, and living in an awareness that enables you to be present and listen authentically with compassion. There is no end game and no graduation as a powerful listener or communicator. This is a lifelong practice, and we will all fall off at times. Success is re-engaging in the process each time we fall off., and always recovering faster than the time before.

Call to Action

My request is that you remain engaged in this practice and join communities of people doing the same. Please reach out if you want additional training or to join a mentorship program where we continue to practice as a community. If you are a sales professional, manager, leader, or coach wanting to deepen your understanding of these and other concepts that will catapult your success, please reach out. If you are an executive and want to enlist services to consult on your corporate culture and communications practices or to provide executive coaching to your employees, please reach out.

Please feel free to reach out to Marcia Martin or another of my mentors. Their contact information may have been included in this book, and if not, reach out to me, and I will help you to connect.

To contact Susan Postnikoff:

Company: **Performance Mastery Consulting, Inc.**
Email: **susan@pmc-team.org**
Website: **www.pmc-team.org**

To contact Marcia Martin:

Email: **info@marciamartin.com**
Website: **www.marciamartin.com**

Resources

1. Thich Nhat Hanh, The Art of Mindful Living: How to Bring Love, Compassion, and Inner Peace into Your Daily Life Audio CD – Publisher: Sounds True, November 1, 2000

2. Alan Cohen, Have You Hugged a Monster Today: How to Win Friends and Lose Fiends – Publisher: John Seymour, January 1, 1984

3. Kay Leigh Hagan, Internal Affairs: A Journal Keeping Workbook for Self-Intimacy – Publisher: HarperSanFrancisco, January 1, 1990

4. Tom Peters, Thriving on Chaos: Handbook for a Management Revolution – Publisher: Alfred A. Knopf, New York, January 1, 2988

5. Tom Peters, Excellence Now: Extreme Humanism – Publisher: Networlding Inc., March 30, 2021

6. Stephen R. Covey, The 8th Habit: From Effectiveness to Greatness – Publisher: Simon & Schuster, November 29, 2005

7. The Mayo Clinic Staff, "Stress Puts Your Health at Risk" as viewed at https://www.mayoclinic.org/healthy-lifestyle/stress-management/in-depth/stress/art-20046037. Publisher: The Mayo Clinic, as viewed July 20, 2023

8. Marcia Martin, MarciaMartin.com and MarciaMartinClub.com, both websites last visited September 5, 2023, plus more than 20 years of handouts from Marcia's live training seminars from 1998 to 2003.

Acknowledgements

First and foremost, the bulk of the content in this book is based on the teachings of Marcia Martin (marciamartin.com). She has been my coach, my mentor, and my friend for more than 20 years. She taught me virtually everything I know about sales and communication. When I am practicing her teachings, I am at my best self personally, and I am most productive professionally. In my early years selling spine implants and capital equipment, I had a doctor tell me that he liked me, but he did not think I was a great sales representative. I started looking for sales training, and at that time, a close friend asked me to attend "Power Speaking, Power Selling" by Marcia Martin. I agreed and became a Marcia Martin groupie, attending training after training, learning everything she had to teach me.

In 2001 I moved to California, where I had become a very successful medical device sales representative. I had been transferred from Canada to California by Medtronic Sofamor Danek (now known simply as Medtronic). In California, Marcia introduced me to her friend - and well-known "The Landmark Forum" leader - Herb Tanzer. Herb passed away a few years ago, but not before adding to Marcia's teachings and shaping me into a corporate trainer. Herb helped me create and lead live training for the Health Industry Distributor's Association (HIDA), for Scripps Healthcare, and for the Orthopedic Research and Education Foundation, which booked me as a speaker geared towards the orthopaedic industry and moderated by a panel of surgeons at the American Academy of Orthopaedic Surgery Annual Meeting in 2005.

Herb also introduced me to the executive team at the American Botanical Pharmacy (ABP) in Marina Del Rey, where I was given my first long-term contract as a trainer of their retail sales team. ABP offered me a full-time position, which unfortunately conflicted with other opportunities at the time. When I first started working with the ABP retail team, they told me the first concern they wanted help with was how to handle all the angry customers. I have always felt that my greatest accomplishment at ABP was training the staff how to 'be', to eliminate "all the angry customers".

Utilizing Marcia's and Herb's training, I was able to help the staff understand how they were responsible for creating or provoking the angry customer and how to shift a customer's mood while politely and confidently standing behind the company's policies. It only took about a month for the staff to no longer experience any angry customers. Those angry customers just magically disappeared when the staff became accountable for their cause in the matter and changed themselves rather than trying to change the customer.

I have also been influenced by my training at the Hypnosis Motivational Institute in Tarzana, California, where I studied Hypnosis and Neuro Linguistic Programming (NLP). Marcia's and Herb's trainings were like a master's degree in NLP, and HMI's training on hypnosis and the interaction between hypnosis and NLP has given me additional perspective and some new skills and insights. I recommend HMI to anyone wanting to study hypnosis, especially if you want to be a professional hypnotherapist. I am currently a Certified Master Hypnotist. The hypnosis training provided insight into human behavior, the function of the human brain, and the relationship between hypnosis and sales and marketing.

Another person who added to my body of knowledge is Michael Sloopka of Guelph, Ontario and his company, Selling Solutions Inc. While I was working for Medtronic Canada, Michael was hired to train the Sofamor Danek Canada distributor sales force on his system for 'Strategic Customer Management', as well as helping our sales team with business planning, and negotiation skills. Mr. Sloopka was so practical and hands-on in his approach that his training included visiting my home office, instructing me on the type of shelving and notebooks to purchase, and teaching me how to organize my office and my business.

To this day, I still utilize a modified version of the business planning process that he provided us with as part of his training, and I still have my Strategic Customer Management binder. I also still maintain a copy of the business plan he helped me create, for which I won an award for the best business plan for my sales territory Sofamor Danek Canada (now known as Medtronic, Canada). Not only did the plan look good, but it had a lofty goal of doubling the sales in my region and producing more than a million dollars in sales. I exceeded the target with a 128% sales increase over the prior year.

There are four authors that have had a profound influence on me. In my early 20s, during that phase of finding out who I was, I came across Internal Affairs, A Journal Keeping Workbook by Katie Leigh Hagan. I still have her book, and there is one simple exercise in her book that I still use regularly. Simplicity is genius. A simple three-line exercise has been one of the most helpful tools in my personal and professional life. "Simplicity is genius" – this, for me, is a mantra. If something can be related in a way that makes it seem simple, then anyone can grasp it and utilize it.

Although I respect professionals who develop mathematically and scientifically complex systems that I could not even start to comprehend, I also believe that if the presentation of a process is too complicated, then the learners will be unlikely to succeed. Great teachers simplify complicated concepts in such a way that their target audience can understand them.

The second author that has influenced me greatly is Thich Nhat Hanh. I was saddened by his passing in January of 2022, and I regret that I never went to a retreat to meet him personally. What I gained from him were meditation exercises that I did not have to sit down or close my eyes to practice. He provided the concept of mindfulness and offered a way of meditation that can be utilized while performing simple but necessary tasks – walking, driving, cleaning - any simple task can be done mindfully as a form of meditation. The practice of meditation in this manner instills mindfulness as a way of operating in life. My absolute favorite exercise from Thich Nhat Hanh is stop-light meditation. Imagine taking hectic Los Angeles traffic and doing an open-eye meditation every time you are stuck waiting at a stoplight. It transforms a stressful drive into an opportunity for calmness and reflection.

In business, I was influenced in 2010 by Stephen R. Covey's **The 8th Habit**. During 2022, as I was writing Empowered Communication on the shirt tails of the Covid-19 fiasco, I found myself drawn to Tom Peter's book Excellence Now: Extreme Humanism. Steven R. Covey first gave us **The 7 Habits of Highly Effective People** and then followed it up with The 8th Habit, where he acknowledged the shift from the Industrial Era with its corporate hierarchies to the Information Age and the need for workforce collaboration rather than top-down direction.

Tom Peters has now provided yet another shift by declaring the era of Extreme Humanism. When we talk about Corporate Culture, a company's culture is generally established by the executive team and board of directors with the intent to produce results and achieve specific goals and objectives. With stockholders and investors to account to, that culture may be very methodical and mechanical. Modern companies usually have a *'cause-marketing'* plan that looks very charitable to potential customers and the public, while all too often, the corporate directive, focus and drive are more comparable to a sweatshop.

Most companies have a culture where emotions and personal issues are expected to be left at home – especially by the top executives and revenue-generating sales teams. Attention tends to be on the bottom line, and it is necessary to demonstrate to the board of directors, investors, and stockholders that their money is being well spent with the return on investment on track as promised. At the same time, I think it's safe to say that most employees would prefer a culture that values extreme humanism.

Tom Peters lays out both objective and subjective data and rationale to explain and support, both scientifically and emotionally, why a corporate culture based on extreme humanism is mandatory if modern corporations are to be successful. Tom implores executives to implement extreme humanism immediately as the best means to achieving excellence. I completely agree.

I often find myself in awe at the serendipity of life, and finding Tom's new book was one of those moments. Here I am, writing a book that brings the 'woo-woo' of transformational training to a structured, science-based audience of Corporate America's C-suite Executives - many of whom are still leading from the mindset they acquired during the industrial era – and Tom Peters made it okay to bring humanism and spirituality into Corporate America. In fact, he pointed out that it is a necessity that corporate American leadership becomes based on extreme humanism.

The book you are now reading, **Empowered Communication: C-Suite & Sales Edition**, will allow you to be an exceptional communicator empowered to create a humanistic corporate culture that is also extremely productive. You will produce results far beyond the expectations of investors, stockholders, and your board of directors, while also showing integrity with your human resource directives, your cause-marketing, and your charitable connections. That humanistic culture starts with your business communication at the executive level, filters down throughout your entire organization, and extends to your employees' families and friends and to your customers' families and friends. Success in business starts with empowered communication.

I also need to acknowledge Robert J. Moore, who made getting this book published a reality. When I was having trouble deciding what to include in the book, he gave me a piece of advice that instantly made the book take shape. I had ideas for several books and could not decide where to start with the first one. Robert clarified that for me, and then – with Robert's guidance – the writing started to flow with grace and ease. Of course, this means that there are more books to follow, so if you like this one, please stay tuned!

About the Author

Susan Postnikoff was born in Saskatchewan, Canada, and lived her first five years on a farm with no running water in one of the harshest climates in the world. Being the person who always found a way to better her situation and to do things differently than the status quo, Susan moved to Toronto part way through her Bachelor of Science degree and then to California a few years into her professional career.

Susan has a unique perspective on… well… everything! She is analytical, creative, engaging, and direct. She has a thirst for knowledge and is always researching, questioning, and evaluating. She is exceptional at contract design and negotiation and was a top performer in medical device sales, with an exceptional skillset for business planning and forecasting. Susan was integral in the launch of several disruptive medical devices and biologics, including stem cell technologies and image-guided surgery and robotics equipment.

As a beach volleyball player and NCCP Level II Coach, Susan has coached high school and club teams and has played in FIVB and AVP Professional Beach Volleyball Tournaments. She also studied NLP and is a Certified Master Hypnotist and Hypnotherapist. Susan has provided career transition coaching, relationship coaching, sales and customer service training, and has consulted on sales and operations integration, and corporate culture shift.

Building Self-Esteem in Teens

Accept Who You Are, Manage Emotions, Become Self-Confident, and Accomplish Your Goals to Be the Person You Want to Be

Scott Douglas

Table of Contents

Introduction

Never bend your head. Always hold it high. Look the world straight in the eye. –
Helen Keller (In T. Gur, *Never Bend Your Head*)

Confidence can be an important weapon, and all the successful people since the beginning of time know how to wield it. Self-confidence comes from your perception of yourself and your "self-belief," and it can be defined "as a feeling of trust in one's abilities, qualities, and judgement" (Norton, 2018). When you find your self-confidence, you will find a whole new world, and it all starts with working on your self-esteem.

I once knew a kid who struggled with his self-esteem and had no confidence at all. He'd wake up every day and take a look in the mirror, hating what he'd see. His appearance, what his voice sounded like, his entire personality—he hated everything. He felt powerless and was miserable. If he laughed, it was for just a moment, then he'd remember that he truly hated the way his laugh sounded. If he was happy for just one second, he'd remember that he didn't deserve it. He couldn't accept any compliments and when someone did have something nice to say about him, he somehow found a way to dismiss it. I'd watch him get bullied because he just wouldn't fight for himself, through words or otherwise. He constantly worried and put himself down. He was hurtling toward a very dark place where nothing in the world could help him.

One day, I shared some of my most valuable strategies with him, which he quietly accepted, and I never saw him for a long time. When I finally met him again recently, he was a completely different person. The first thing I noticed was that he had the biggest smile on his face and his entire demeanor had changed. Even though he went through the toughest time back then, he was a thriving, confident person now. Unbeknownst to me, he had taken everything I had offered him and implemented it steadfastly in his life. His story of resilience and strength in the face of challenges is incredible, and his gratitude was humbling.

If you're a teenager like him who has felt self-doubt weighing you down for as long as you can remember, and you just want the feeling of confidence so you can be happier, more carefree, and have the ability to chase your dreams, then this book is going to be a game-changer. This isn't just any other ordinary self-help book. This is going to be your companion and mentor as you take the journey to the well-deserved freedom you're looking for. This book has a unique and holistic approach that will bridge the role of parents and children in the development of self-esteem.

This book will have a seven-step framework and practical guide that will help parents and teens to understand what they're going through, and combat it effectively. This is your comprehensive roadmap with everything you need to guide you through the journey of enriching your self-esteem. If you struggle with body image issues, academic pressure, bullying, peer pressure, expectations from your parents, or perfectionist tendencies, you will find strategies you can use to improve your life.

Once you have mastered the seven-step road map, you will have developed important skills such as being aware of yourself, through understanding your emotions, actions, and relationships. You will develop self-awareness, which is an important foundation to build self-esteem. Cultivating self-awareness will teach you how to love yourself, regardless of what you look like or what society says you should be. Nothing will stand in your way of being self-compassionate and learning to be kind and gentle with yourself. You will be a master of destroying self-criticism and negative self-talk, and you will learn how to motivate yourself. You will learn the crucial steps toward emotional resilience so that you can accept change and cope with any stressful event that happens in your life.

Self-acceptance will become second nature to you. Your self-worth will increase, allowing you to gain confidence in your abilities. You will feel good about yourself holistically. One of the most important steps in the framework is learning to cultivate healthy relationships, which will guide and teach you everything that you need to know about improving your relationships and turning the unhealthy ones into ones that are good for you. You will learn some important strategies and tips for conflict resolution and communication, such as how to set boundaries that are important for your mental health and learning to be empathetic. The most important step that you will learn is to stand up for yourself. You will discover strategies to deal with peer pressure and bullying, and techniques to help you change your perspective and stand up for yourself.

Are you a parent who can see the pain in your kid's eyes every day? You can probably already see what their low self-esteem is doing to their life, and you can already see that their lack of self-worth is affecting their relationships negatively. Their school life probably isn't going very well, they seem unhappy more often than not, and they just seem unhappy in general. This is your chance for empowerment and motivation. This might seem like a mammoth task—huge and impossible—but with the strategies and tips in this book, you will find a path that's simple and effective.

You will discover the way to unlock your self-confidence and improve your self-esteem. You will find everything you need to know about recognizing the signs and symptoms of low self-esteem, a breakdown of its causes, what issues to look out for, and most importantly, you will discover how to fight it to give your child the happy and healthy life they need. It's going to be an amazing feeling when you see the confidence in their body language, their new ability to take positive risks, and getting out of their comfort zone. They will be calmer, more focused, and achieve what they set out to do. Here's to a beautiful journey through breaking free of low self-esteem, accepting who you are, learning to manage your emotions, becoming self-confident, and accomplishing your goals. You can do this!

Self-Esteem: The Building Blocks and Puzzle Pieces

As soon as you trust yourself, you will know how to live. –Johann Wolfgang von Goethe

Trusting yourself is a significant aspect of conquering self-esteem, and to get there, you need to first have a comprehensive understanding of the idea behind self-esteem and the role that it plays in your personal development. Self-esteem will carry you through all of life's challenges, and it is the basis of who you are and your sense of self. If you understand self-esteem, you will be able to learn how to be more self-assured, which is a critical aspect of being able to function to your fullest potential. This chapter lays out this important concept and its influence on who you are, how you see yourself, and the world around you. We will dive into the psychology behind self-esteem and what it is at its very core to pave the way toward learning the strategies to improve it.

What Is Self-Esteem?

Simply explained, self-esteem refers to your view of value and worth. It "describes your level of confidence in your abilities and attributes" and when your self-esteem is good, your "overall quality of life" is improved too (Cherry, 2022). Low self-esteem means that you will be demotivated in different areas of your life, and this will eventually affect your mental health negatively. Our self-esteem depends on "our opinions and beliefs about ourselves," and these are aspects that are not so easy to change (Mind, 2022). It's molded by your thoughts, the relationships you have, and your various life experiences.

Breaking It Down

According to psychotherapist Dr. Joe Accardi (2022), good self-esteem is created through 10 important elements. If you are able to cultivate a few of these attributes, you will be a step closer to creating a foundation of optimism to nurture positive self-esteem that will remain with you throughout your life (Accardi, 2022):

- The first element is the feeling of **personal and interpersonal security**. Dr. Accardi says that a child needs to feel safe and secure in all ways that exist, such as in their "familial relationships, home environment, themselves, and their potential future."

- The second element is the sense of **social belonging**. You might already know how important this quality is, especially when it comes to your kids' friendships and acquaintances. Your child needs to feel secure and accepted in most of the social environments they are part of, such as friend groups in school, religious gatherings, extracurricular groups like school bands or sports teams, and even other family members. Children who are accepted and feel loved or valued by these groups usually have better self-esteem.

- The element of **trust** is the next important one and as mentioned at the beginning of the chapter, trust will help you conquer self-esteem issues. You need to be able to trust people but also have that feeling returned to you. As a parent, letting your child know that you trust them plays a massive role in getting them to trust themselves. The easiest way to do this is to make sure you give them the chance to discover this by giving them some responsibility that you know they are capable of handling safely. In this way, they will learn to trust themselves to complete the task and be independent. Of course, you need to remember to give them the space to finish the task without constantly checking up on them. For them to trust you, never go back on your word.